THE WAYWARD WAY

The Power in Wilderness Journeys

TAYLOR FIELD

NEW HOPE®
PUBLISHERS

Birmingham, Alabama

New Hope® Publishers
5184 Caldwell Mill Rd.
St. 204-221
Hoover, AL 35244
NewHopePublishers.com
New Hope Publishers is a division of Iron Stream Media.

New Hope Publishers serves its authors as they express their views, which
may not express the views of the publisher.

Library of Congress Cataloging-in-Publication Data

Names: Field, Taylor, author.
Title: The wayward way : the power in wilderness journeys / Taylor Field.
Description: First [edition]. | Birmingham : New Hope Publishers, 2017.
Identifiers: LCCN 2017041984 | ISBN 9781625915382 (permabind)
Subjects: LCSH: Wilderness (Theology) | Spiritual life—Christianity.
Classification: LCC BV4509.5 .F446 2017 | DDC 248.2—dc23
LC record available at https://lccn.loc.gov/2017041984

ISBN-13: 978-1-62591-538-2

N184111 • 0218 • 1.5M1

"Taylor has done it again—taking the real world and demonstrating from the ancients that we are not the first to struggle with broken dreams. This is not a book of pat answers but one with which all can identify, and then learn how to keep walking. The present is not our destination."

—Gary D. Chapman, Ph.D.,
author of *The Five Love Languages*

"If you open this book with a humble heart, God will use Taylor to teach you lessons that you will never forget, that you need to hear, and that will strengthen you for whatever 'wilderness' you are facing or are about to face."

—Kerrick Thomas,
pastor of The Journey Church NYC

"Taylor Field has worked with the North American Mission Board for more than thirty years and is currently serving with Send Relief Inc., the compassion ministry of NAMB. He has spent a great deal of time in compassion ministries and brings encouragement through personal experiences into his new book. Taylor personally models compassion ministry daily in Lower Manhattan."

—David Melber,
vice president, Send Relief,
North American Mission Board

"Taylor has been a model in NYC not just for church planting but also for having a legacy of faithfulness as a Christian leader. With all the challenges of pioneering a ministry-minded church in the city and all the challenges of leading ourselves, Pastor Taylor Field is the man who can help guide us as we navigate our wilderness. Read this book and let him, along with the Holy Spirit, be your guide."

—James Roberson,
lead pastor, Bridge Church NYC

For Eric — Thanks for helping me through a wilderness or two. Taylor

DEDICATION

To all those who feel they have failed but haven't.

Other Books by Taylor Field

Upside-Down Devotion: Extreme Action for a Remarkable God

Upside-Down Freedom: Inverted Principles for Christian Living

Upside-Down Leadership: Rethinking Influence and Success

A Church Called Graffiti: Finding Grace on the Lower East Side

Mercy Streets: Seeing Grace on the Streets of New York

Squat: A Novel

CONTENTS

THE WAYWARD WAY

The golden key or endless wrath,

I see no guarantees.

A signless sign, a pathless path,

a vane without a breeze.

A wilderness turned upside down,

It's here—you didn't chose it,

The fruitful way has all turned brown,

You find it when you lose it.

All great works were prepared in the desert,
including the redemption of the world.

—A. G. Sertillanges

THE WILDERNESS AS PARADOX

The golden rule is that there is no golden rule.

—George Bernard Shaw

Now look what you have done. Your hopes were so high. You had so much going for you. But you had such a hot head and outraged heart. You were so sure you had it all figured out. You thought you could change the world, but your pride and your anger just made you look foolish. So here you are on the run from everyone, and everyone seems to be running after you. This isn't the kind of place you grew up in. You don't know the ropes. No more comforts here—it's harsh and dry. No one is looking out for you now. If you don't pay close attention, you might die. But you can't go back. You will never go home again. Welcome to your new bleak, dreary, rocky world. Where are you? You are in the wilderness. Way to go, Moses.

Not So Golden After All

It's not that the formulas you learned about life don't work; it's that they don't always work. It's not that the principles don't make sense. It's that some circumstances seem outside those principles. It's not that your assertions aren't true—they are. It's that the world is smaller and larger and more extreme than you ever imagined.

So here is the point of the book—if you can't avoid the wilderness, understand it. If you are not already in it, it is probably coming sometime. If you spend all your efforts attempting to avoid the wilderness completely, you only end up in a more cosmic, endless wilderness. We try so hard to skip the wilderness when we have so many resources right under our noses that could help us understand it.

In actuality, we know intuitively that aimlessness often precedes purpose. Moses understood this, eventually. He spent longer than just about anybody in the wilderness . . . twice.

A wilderness is an empty, pathless, uncultivated region, often a desert. Wilderness eventually came to represent any bewildering situation or time—often a time when the normal comforts are stripped away. So it's a place, but it is also a state of mind. People may not know the story of Moses, but they still use the word *wilderness* all the time. The idea of the wilderness runs through our lives, and it runs all through the Bible.

Even if we haven't recently read the ancient story of Moses's anger as an Egyptian prince, his murder of an Egyptian, and the necessity of escaping into the desert next to Egypt, the concept of the wilderness still soaks our culture. It's possible we might even use the word sometimes, but the idea itself is so very common we don't think about it, much. Until we are in it.

The wilderness is that place where things don't seem to be the way they used to be. The old formulas you lived by don't seem to work anymore. The golden rule you thought you knew, whatever it was in your personal life, doesn't seem so golden after all. Moses was a prince, highly educated in the ways of Egyptian civilization. He knew the ways of the world and how to exercise power. He found himself a runaway, in a land with different norms. In this kind of situation, you often don't need just to learn. You also need to unlearn.

MULTIPLE BLOWS

The wilderness of the Bible is a place. But wilderness can take a lot of other forms too. Usually the wilderness experience is precipitated by some change. Your lose your job, your spouse leaves you or passes away, you wake up to the dreary prospect of unending depression, you get ignored for that promotion, you get a horrible diagnosis, you get arrested, you have to go to rehab, your application is rejected, you find yourself trapped in some circumstances that never seem to end.

As a pastor who has worked with homeless people for nearly forty years, I notice a pattern in some of the people I worked with. Some of them functioned pretty well in society for a while, but the problem was that they felt as though they were hit by more than one crisis at a time.

For example, maybe you come home from your job to find an eviction notice on your door and a note inside that your spouse has left you. Or you lose your job, and on the way home, you get hit by a car. Or you get expelled from school, and you get kicked out of the house. It's receiving more than one punch at a time that pushes you over the edge. The wilderness comes when the world as you know it has simply fallen apart and hit you with blow after blow. Moses, for example, kills a man and his deed is known. Suddenly, he loses his home, his family, his possessions, and his status.

Or consider the man sitting on a park bench with a small bag containing his possessions. He tried to find a place on the bench where the sun shone. His daughter had died of cancer. His wife had eventually killed herself. The people at his work were understanding, but as his drug use accelerated, they had to let him go. He shuffled from park to park, sleeping on subways, trying to keep clean, reading the sports pages. He got food from trashcans, mission churches, and Hare Krishnas. He kept his own counsel. Well-meaning people kept telling him what he needed to do. He knew he was in an in-between time, he just didn't know what the next step might be.

What precipitates the wilderness can be large or small. Whatever the circumstances, the wilderness forces you to leave the comfort of your old ways and your old thoughts. It's a crazy time. The wilderness has the word *wild* right in it. What normally comforts you is not there. You may discover you are not who you thought you were. And neither is God. You doubt your sanity. In your previous life, you built little temples. In the wilderness, those temples are gone, or seem irrelevant. On the other hand, you may find a burning bush when you were not looking for it. It's all so different and not necessarily safe—a bush that burns could also burn you.

Some people may talk about what they learned in the wilderness, but not many people really like to be in the wilderness. That's what makes it so hard. At the sight of this barren place, our tidy little concepts about life are gone. In the wilderness, the sky reaches down to the bleak horizon and grips it like teeth on a bone. The wind boxes your ears and closes your mouth and only makes you more thirsty and tired. The howl in the night could be a stray dog, but it is probably the first of a pack of wolves. They are not on your side.

Here's one of the biggest challenges with the wilderness: when you are in it, you often don't know how long it will last. Maybe it will never end. Or maybe you will find a border to the badlands tomorrow, and you will be home for supper. There may be fruitfulness in this desert, but you don't know that when you are in the middle of it. Often when you are in the middle of a dark time, it feels as though it will last forever.

Maybe in the beginning you thought following God would bring abundance, but somehow you find yourself in this place where nothing seems to grow. Nothing. All the promises seem broken. The purpose has vanished. Everything is so upside down from what you expected.

THE QUESTION-LESS WORLD

Our culture used to talk about this stuff—being in a time of wilderness—often. Poets call this experience a wasteland. Philosophers talk about existential angst. Psychologists talk about a midlife crisis. Mystics talk about the dark night of the soul. Hardcore hikers talk about the hard things one learns in the wild in order to develop a survival attitude. Churchgoers talk about that long dry spell in their spiritual journeys.

Yes, being in the wilderness can be a state of mind rather than a place. But wilderness journeys in the Bible often come from a person in a real desert. It's strange that some Christians who treasure the Bible the most seem the most obtuse about what happens in the wilderness. Why is that?

We want to short-circuit the wilderness time. We want to go from a confining experience directly to the Promised Land in one easy step—instant freedom and purpose, with no wandering. Perhaps this is part of our problem. Maybe the desire to skip this part of life, even if well intentioned, is what makes our quick judgments seem so out of touch and glib to others.

How strange that Bible readers have forgotten what everyone else in the world has been talking about. For when we return to the Bible, we find that in actuality almost everyone seems to go to the desert at some point—Abraham, Sarah, Hagar, Jacob, Moses, David, Jesus, and Paul, to name a few.

Here's one of the great ironies of our time. We who take the Bible seriously have become rightly known as the ones with the answers. It's true—the Bible shows us the meaning and purpose of life—real answers. But somehow in the process we became known as the ones with merely pat answers, formulaic principles, and even pig-headed views. Currently many of our answers don't seem to fit anymore—for others . . . or even for ourselves. Maybe we have forgotten that with all the answers in the Bible, the characters in the Bible are also the ones who bring the hardest questions.

We carry a Bible around proclaiming its answers, forgetting that the same book carries all the resources to walk with us through the chaotic and random suffering that seems to be a part of life. For example, right in the middle of our Bible, we have the long Book of Job. It is a book filled with tortured inquiry. We often malign Job's friends for being unfeeling and preachy. But as we read the book, we find Job's friends are really the ones with all the well-intentioned answers. Some of their answers sound pretty good. They are trying to help.

It is Job who has all kinds of questions in the middle of his struggle. It is only Job's friends who live in this different world—a confident, question-less world. Job, on the other hand, is in another kind of place altogether, a place of seeking and pain and disorder and injustice and challenge. Being surrounded by his friends who have all the answers only makes things worse. He sits on the ash heap and lives in a place of chaotic anguish—a sort of inner lonely wilderness.

Or we turn to Psalms, where agony and confusion look to be the other side of praise.

Or we turn to Lamentations, where Jeremiah gropes through a seemingly endless tunnel of depression, with only a few sparks of hope rising from the dark.

Or we turn to the heart of the gospel, which is the crucifixion of a Man who is not only divine but also fully human. Putting aside the cosmic dimensions of His sacrifice, we still hear a Man, nailed and naked, crying out to God, asking why God has forsaken Him. The question is so important that the Gospel writers repeated it to us in the original Aramaic.

So here is the irony. We as Christians get tagged as the ones with superficial pat answers when we in actuality we uphold a book full of all kinds of people who walk through the chaos of suffering and purposelessness. That chaos is often called the wilderness. And in that wilderness, the Bible shows people whose apparent purpose has been turned upside down. Let us not overlook what those who have gone before us have learned.

VERTIGO

Take Job's friends, the poster children for giving the pat answers. But Job's friends had some meaningful responses that explained what was happening, at least in their minds. They could talk about God's ways with assurance. But the wilderness experience keeps us from intellectualizing God the way Job's friends did. In those lonely, distorted times, we can no longer treat God as a concept, as something to argue about. God is not just a set of principles. The story of Job reminds us of truth when we get too sermonic. Job is in a different kind of place.

Here's one way to think about it—imagine you are on the edge of a vast desert. The wind blows across the arid rocks and roars in your ears. You find yourself on the rim of a high cliff. You are not sure whether you should climb or descend. You don't have a foothold. You reach for a branch growing out of a rock to steady yourself. The branch gives way. You slip. You look up and you look down. Your world is turning upside down. You feel dizzy.

This is the way a pastor described experiencing God in the wilderness times. The pastor isn't from our generation, nor from the generation just preceding us. Gregory of Nyssa, a brilliant pastor who lived 1,600 years ago, described wilderness times this way. He said experiencing God is more like being on the extreme edge of a very high cliff in a lonely and wild place. Sometimes experiencing God is more like dizziness, even vertigo. We thought we knew the way. Now everything is on the line, and the vastness and strangeness of it all blows away all our little tidy conceptions. In the wilderness, things are more terrible, and maybe more grand, than we imagined. This is what heading for the wilderness does. In getting closer to God, you may lose your balance. Forget your neat, doctrinal answers. You thought you knew the way. So did Moses. Get ready for the vertigo.

Of course, in an upside-down way, there is value in the wilderness of that vertigo because perhaps you are seeing more of life than you did before. At least our perceptions are different. Eventually, you become someone different too. Sometimes a shocking fruitfulness is on the other side of the wilderness. Or you find an ability to connect with others in a way you never had before.

But when you are in the desert, the problem is having no map, no path, not even a firm foundation to stand on. The difficulties and uncertainties in our circumstances feel as though they may go on without any closure, at least without the kind of closure we yearn for.

It is easy to write about the wilderness while sitting safely in my house with my little cup of coffee and my self-satisfied sense of well-being. I can easily tell people what they ought to feel. I can write about the assurance of a fruitful ending to the story. But in the wilderness, there are few guarantees.

To be honest, in real life, we have all seen people go into the wilderness, get overwhelmed, and never return. Ministering in New York City, I have seen this happen many times.

Because of all that unpleasant uncertainty and real danger, our own tendency is to jump past the wild experience of dryness and bleakness, to skip it if we can. Given what it is like, who wouldn't want to skip it? But when we try to skip it, we tend to deny it. Remaining in that desert is often so unpleasant we are rarely able to see the benefits that can come from staying. Long afterward, people can attest to the inner work God was doing in them and their gratitude at not getting out of the wilderness too soon. But usually only long afterward.

Most change is a kind of death, and we want to move right from the death of the old to the clear abundance and purpose of the next stage. Many of us find it hard to live for long in the uncertain and the indeterminate—understandably so. We may try to force a closure—for ourselves and also for others—and by doing so we ignore what is happening.

If we can't find a way to understand our uncertainty, we might create our own way to put the confusing pieces together too soon. Being in the wilderness opens a window to our life, and it is a window we often don't understand. We feel we need a pattern, a paradigm. It's the same reason we may search the craters on the face of the moon to find the image of an old man or a rabbit or something else. That's human nature; that's how we survive. But in the tough times, we see in a different way, and perhaps we begin to see that maybe there is no simple pattern where we thought there was. The man in the moon is not a man in the moon after all but something far more intricate from what the children's stories told us.

THE RIVER THAT IS NOT A RIVER

My apartment is next to the East River in New York City. For years, as I walked along the river, I absentmindedly tried to figure out the direction of the current. Simple enough, I thought. I would look down into the deep, dark water, swirling around the abutments of the bridge. But things didn't make sense. Sometimes the river seemed to flow one way, and then sometimes it seemed to flow the other way. Sometimes the water seemed to swirl both ways. This just couldn't be. Why in the world didn't the current flow in one direction—that's what a river does, right? Why didn't it do what it was supposed to do?

But I finally asked some questions and learned that the current is not the kind of current that flows in one direction in this river. In fact, the river is not even a river at all. The East River is really what they call a tidal strait, a part of the ocean that just looks like a river, but is subject to the pull of the ocean, high tides, low tides, the moon, and forces of gravity I could hardly imagine or explain.

I thought it was a river. I was sure it was a river. I was confident it should flow in one direction. But it didn't. In reality, there were great influences pulling on that water that I had not ever considered.

Life is like that. We think things should flow one way, and one day, without explanation, things flow another way. We think we are looking at a river, but it is really something much more expansive. We thought we had it all figured out. We had our rules and principles, but they don't seem to fit our experience any more. We may want to jump to the conclusion that there are no rules or principles, but that would be a mistake too.

THE PLACE OF SCORPIONS AND THIRSTY GROUND

The wilderness in the Bible is the kind of place that changes us. In fact, the wilderness, or desert, is part of the bloodstream of the biblical world. Even the title of one of the books of the Bible, Numbers, is translated "in the desert" from the Hebrew. So Numbers refers to that forty years in the wilderness we have heard so much about—really just one of many wilderness experiences in the Bible. Those forty years were not even Moses's first experience in the wilderness.

When the Bible talks about the wilderness, what is it like? The words *wilderness* and *desert* are used to mean arid and semiarid places, sandy deserts, rocky plateaus, an empty place, uninhabited:

1. From a practical standpoint, it is an unproductive place where you are alone. In the wilderness, we are led "in a land of deserts and pits, in a land of drought and deep darkness, in a land that no one passes through, where no man dwells" (Jeremiah 2:6). It is a wasteland, and we will use the words *wilderness* and *desert* interchangeably here.

2. In the biblical world, the wilderness is a wild place. It is a place "great and terrifying . . . with its fiery serpents and scorpions and thirsty ground where there was no water" (Deuteronomy 8:15). Anything can happen there—some things that are very bad or maybe very good. You could lose your way or find your calling.

3. It is the place where God can "speak tenderly" to us (Hosea 2:14). When we look back on it, it's possible to see it as a place where we found grace, rest, and sight to see God's everlasting love in a deeper sense (Jeremiah 31:2–3). The wilderness can be the place where you hear the voice of an angel, as Hagar did (Genesis 16), or see something that is not normal, like burning bush, as Moses did (Exodus 3).

4. It is often the place where you wander, where you don't know the way, where there are no roads, where in fact you are in danger of dying. "Some wandered in desert wastes, finding no way to a city to dwell in; hungry and thirsty, their soul fainted within them" (Psalm 107:4–5). There are no maps. There are no markers. As mentioned, the wandering in the Bible can be a time of learning and sometimes unlearning—a realization that your previously successful coping tactics for life don't work anymore. Perhaps those clever strategies have simply become irrelevant.

5. It's not a comfortable place, and we so love comfort. We normally don't like being in the wilderness at the time, though we often look back with muted gratitude.

6. We are humbled and tested in the waste places (Deuteronomy 8:2). Things seem uncertain, transitional—we don't know which way to go. We simply don't know when it will end. Are we in a mini-wilderness or one that will last for decades—or a lifetime?

7. The Bible makes it clear that the wilderness is not an ultimate goal. We begin in a garden, the Garden of Eden. We end in a city, the city of God. The wilderness is not forever.

8. The desert place can be the place of radical personal choices too. One can either become bitter, as the

people became with Moses (see Exodus 16, for example), or one can turn to praise, as David did as he fled from his broken, hostile world (Psalm 63).

9.   Sometimes people go into the wilderness more than once. Moses went alone and then again with the liberated Israelites. David was in the wilderness on the run from King Saul as a young man, and then he went again as an older man on the run from his son Absalom. Hagar was driven to the wilderness twice because of her son Ishmael.

Maybe the wilderness is likewise inescapable in our own lives. It means more than a place. We may call it a desert, a dry period, a kind of depression, a wasteland, a dark night of the soul, a midlife crisis, a dark wood, a time of grieving after failure, or something else. But we often have no idea how to escape it. So instead of fighting the wilderness, why not be still and seek to recognize it?

Eugene Peterson, the pastor and translator of *The Message* Bible, updates our understanding of wilderness experiences in his devotional *God's Message for Each Day*:

> Everything is going along fine: we've gotten a job, decorated the house, signed up for car payments. And then suddenly there's a radical change in our bodies, or our emotions, or our thinking, or our friends, or our job. We're out of control. We're in wilderness.

THE MASTER OF PARADOX

So how can we be still and understand the wilderness? Are there tools we can develop in order to appreciate and accommodate what is happening? There are. One of the ways people in the past came to terms with the wild places in life was through the ancient concept of paradox. In other words, the desert is a very dry place, and yet surprisingly, a very fruitful place—both at the same time. Life is like that—paradoxical. Paradoxes turn our thinking upside down, so that we, in effect, can see things right side up.

A paradox is a statement that seems contradictory. It literally means "beyond belief." It is two truths placed side by side that don't seem to be compatible. It is one of the main tools Jesus uses. Jesus is the master of paradox. Overused, paradox can be tedious. But paradox is still a useful form because it can communicate in a new way a truth that has been neglected. By putting things in an unexpected way, a paradox can draw attention to what is usually disregarded.

A paradox doesn't really communicate something new. By presenting things in a special contradictory manner, it simply communicates something that has always been there but seems new.

Jesus told His followers that the one who saves his life will lose it, and the one who loses his life for God's sake will save it (Luke 17:33). The one who would be master must be servant of all (Mark 10:44). Winners become losers (the first shall be last) and losers become winners (the last shall be first—Matthew 20:16). His seemingly contradictory words jump out everywhere once we think about it. Whoever exalts himself will be humbled and vice versa (Luke 14:11). And wouldn't you know it? The least will be the greatest (Luke 9:48).

The Beatitudes in Matthew 5 are sometimes called "the paradoxes of Christ." We may have memorized them as children, but in reality these blessings almost say, "Happy are the unhappy." How odd, even disturbing. Yet we know Jesus had just spent an intense time of prayer and testing before He spoke these words. According to the Bible, He had recently been in a desert.

In the end, Jesus Himself is a living paradox. He went to the desert and came out in richness. He made Himself poor so that we could become rich. He asked for followers but spoke in riddles. He acted as a servant and spoke as a king. He said to turn the other cheek if someone hit you, and He brandished a whip in the Temple. He is the one who brings the true peace of God and was also the one heard crying, "My God, my God, why have you forsaken me?" (Matthew 27: 46). He is the victorious lion who is also the wounded lamb. He is the figure of power who is killed and humiliated as a criminal and yet somehow, through that defeat, achieves victory. He defies categories.

By inverting our views about God and life, by turning them upside down, Jesus was able to help us see what we could not see before. It was always there. We just hadn't seen it. Maybe things have always been like that. Contradictory truths exist side by side, swirling around like the waters of the East River, flowing both ways when we think they should flow just one way. When we forget that contradictory truths exist together and only cling to one side of a formula, we flatten the world because the world is full of experiences that don't flow the way we thought they would. If we don't recognize the contradictions, we become flat ourselves—two-dimensional. In the end, paradox is our friend.

The wilderness in the Bible is the epitome of paradox— dry and deserted, yet in the end it is abundant. It indicates wandering without a purpose, and yet from the experience, a new kind of purpose emerges.

In this short book, we will live in paradox. We will see how failure leads to success and success often leads to failure in the wilderness. In the first three principles outlined in the book, we will see how moving toward dishonor, invisibility, and smallness lead to something more. In the next three principles, we will walk through winding down, giving up, and failing—these things lead to another kind of richness. In the last four principles, we will walk into the in-between times, stop forcing things to happen, and eventually find a different vision where emptiness becomes fullness. In the end, the desert experience helps us understand more fully both our own process as we grow and our ultimate address—the place God has for us.

Is There Anyone Out There in the Storm?

So the wilderness has this way of helping invert things. We can't run from it. We think the wilderness is all dryness, but it turns out to be both fertile and beneficial. We think the desert brings loneliness, but it turns out to bring a new kind of communion. We think the rocky places are an impediment, but they turn into stepping stones. The wilderness, with all its unconscionable pain, can turn things upside down into an inexplicable joy so that perhaps we can see things right side up once again or for the first time.

The desert times become a place of emptiness and sometimes a place of understanding. It can be the place we see God differently. Rather than someone or something we are looking for, God sometimes comes to us in those purposeless places, the wandering places where we don't know where to go.

Just when we think we have some new categories about the wilderness itself, Jesus inverts those categories too. Maybe it's more like the true story of David Churchill, a firefighter from California. In 2013, *Guideposts* reported on the story of a search party David was part of in his area. The party worked hard all day, looking systematically for a lost three-year-old boy, each searcher responsible for a specific part of the diagrammed land. One searcher saw the giant paw print of a mountain lion—not good.

As the search progressed, cold rain began to move in and nightfall was fast approaching. Mist and rain diminished the searchers' visions, and they were slipping on the rocks. The searchers got wetter and wetter and hungrier and hungrier—with no results. They had called out the child's name all day with no answer.

The rain, so difficult for the searchers, simply made David wonder more what the three-year-old must be experiencing, if he were still alive. He worked his way along the path as the storm moved in. But then he decided to do something different.

David simply prayed for guidance. He sensed God leading him to a place where they had already searched. He felt a quiet confidence he hadn't felt all day. As he walked in that area they had already searched, he heard a tiny, faint cry. There he was, his clothes blending in with the background—this little boy, terrified, hungry, and thirsty. David took the little boy in his arms, gave him a granola bar, which the little boy consumed in gulps, and some water. Then David carried him home.

In the same way, Jesus told an unusual story about a lost sheep (Luke 15). Jesus knew what it was like to wander in a wilderness with no pathway. He did that Himself for forty long days. Yet in the story He told, He presented the wilderness differently. The lost lamb is out in the wild and does not know what to look for. But the shepherd is out there in the wild too.

In a way, the shepherd has left common sense. He left the majority of his sheep when common sense would say to call off the search and protect what you have. The shepherd goes back into the wilderness, leaving the comfort of personal rest. He takes the impractical view and risked losing everything—his whole herd, his own life—all for that one, little lost creature.

In our own lives, when we are in the middle of a wilderness time, we sometimes feel abandoned, even betrayed, while looking for God. We may feel empty, cold, and forsaken, with about as much sense and reasoning power as a three-year-old.

But Jesus tells us a little story that, in a way, reframes the way we look at things. In Jesus' story, it is really the Lord who is in the wilderness when everyone else has given up looking for us. Like David Churchill, God is out there in the discomfort and the storm, against all practical odds, in the dark, when those with common sense have shrugged their shoulders and given up. But he was there all the time, seeking us. In comparison, we have about as much understanding as that three-year-old. We just didn't really know.

> ## TAKEAWAY:
>
> If you can't avoid the wilderness, understand it.
>
> Many characters in the Bible go through times of wilderness and wandering.
>
> We can come to terms with the wilderness through the use of paradox.
>
> Jesus reframes the idea of the lonely wilderness.

1

HONORING
DISHONOR

I have seen the moment of my greatness flicker,
I have seen the eternal footman hold my coat,
and snicker.

—T. S. Eliot,
"The Love Song of J. Alfred Prufrock"

Once you were a king. But now your world has imploded. All you thought you needed was just a little respect. But now you are nothing. You are worse than nothing. You are a negative nothing. Because there's someone over there who is even making fun of you. Throwing stones at you. Cursing you. Retelling your story in the worst possible light. Reminding you of your past failures.

And, actually, the accuser's words are true. Since you've lost everything, all you can do is trudge along and listen to the cursing, words that remind you of all your defeats. And you're not that young anymore, either. Maybe this time you are too old to rebuild, to start again.

Worst of all, someone you loved was the one who hurt you so deeply, who crushed you in front of others. It wasn't some enemy. It was one of your own. Your family knew your problems. You never seemed that great to them. You have nothing now, not even any shoes. And nothing but barrenness and uncertainty lie ahead. You are going into the wilderness again. Way to go, David. Once you were a king.

THROWING STONES

This chapter is about humiliation. It really is the dishonor of the thing. The disrespect. Humiliation is worse than physical blows. King David in this story is no longer a young man. He has been through a lot. And here is this guy, this cursing, shouting guy, following David's ignoble retreat from his palace, pointing out his failure. It's unbelievable. David's world had fallen apart, betrayed and humiliated by his own son. David left his world in shambles, weeping and barefoot in grief. And here was this guy, this guy named Shimei, walking along beside him, cursing "continually," pointing out his bungling, his guilt, his shame.

Shimei was throwing stones. No, not metaphorically. He was literally throwing stones at the "former" king and at the ones who were with him. This was insufferable. Of course, a member of David's party sought permission to do the obvious in such circumstances. The man asked if he could go over and chop off Shimei's head. But David refused this temporary vindication. He was heading toward the wilderness (2 Samuel 16:5–14).

I once had what I thought was a brilliant idea for empowering those who were hungry in my church's neighborhood. I have worked for more than thirty years with a church that started in a storefront in the Lower East Side of Manhattan in New York City. We still call our church a mission in order to emphasize our calling to express Christ's love in tangible ways. People came to our mission for food all the time, and we were often able to help provide something for them. My wonderful idea was that we would all gather together and work for an hour and then gratefully eat food together, feeling the deep satisfaction of a job completed.

We purposefully gave each person a set of gloves with a number on it in order to keep people organized into groups. They also received a bag to pick up trash in our park. The whole endeavor was well designed. Team leaders would go out with the more than one-hundred workers and their carefully numbered gloves and clean up our neighborhood. Then we would gather together for a communal meal, with that special gratification of having done meaningful work for the community.

For a number of reasons, the plan was a train wreck before it started. People threw their gloves down, shouted, and got angry with their team leaders. We stopped doing it after a couple of weeks.

Some of the people in our neighborhood harbored residual resentment. One man, who had lived on the street for a long time, picked me out for his particular ire. For the next two years, two whole years, every time he saw me on the street, he would follow me and curse me out, foamy spit flying from his mouth. He would shout nasty things and lace his curses with attacks on me for taking advantage of the poor, trying to profit off those suffering, and exploiting people's poverty. He would walk right beside me, or just behind me, pointing his finger at me, crying out like a prophet to the neighborhood.

Honestly, it's very hard to maintain a reputation as a respected pastor of the community, humbly helping the poor, when you have this individual following you around furiously cursing you as you walk along the sidewalk. Unlike David, I was often ready to give the instructions to chop his head off, anything to stop the public humiliation. I didn't go to the desert, but for two years, the illusion of my so-called "respectability" was totally gone.

WHAT HAPPENED TO ALL THAT RESPECT?

Winston Churchill knew about the loss of respectability. He was no stranger to adventure and honor. Honor was extremely important to him. As a young man, he was in the last cavalry charge of the British Empire. Later he was captured in the Second Boer War and escaped and became famous, writing about his exploits. He was for a time the First Lord of the Admiralty in World War I. In his middle age, he was a leading politician in British politics, being, among other things, the monetary chancellor. He was held in great esteem.

Then his party was swept out of office in the general election in Great Britain, and so was he. At that time, he lost most of his money in the stock market crash of 1929. In addition, he was hit by a car and had a terrible physical injury. Churchill believed his career was over. From the age of 55 to the age of 65, his years of influence seemed lost. He was old and out of sync with his time. Other leaders felt he was out of date.

He stood up for King Edward VIII when the political forces were against him, which left Churchill subject to a flood of abuse. He was not a fan of Gandhi, a rising star in the political world. He talked of the danger of Germany when everyone longed for peace. At one point, the House of Commons would not even let Churchill speak. Some would call that a deep humiliation. He was often excoriated by the press.

This period is referred to as Churchill's wilderness years. It was a time of lost influence after WWI and before his return to power in WWII.

We understand a little. It is not the money. It is not the loss of influence. It is the indignity of the thing. It is the lack of respect. We are working hard and we are gossiped about. People see the worst of motives in what we do. We have less and less shreds of dignity. We stand in a group, awkwardly, and we are ignored. Then the attacks come. Our best intentions are interpreted as evil. People are unsupportive. This can be how the wilderness can feel.

Even modern politics can refer to the wilderness years, but the concept is much deeper than that. We can also talk about the wilderness as a desert, a place with no rain and very few people. One feels a certain kind of loneliness.

When we are humiliated or shamed, we sometimes withdraw or, more often, are forced to withdraw. We often go to what feels like an empty place. What causes us to withdraw? Maybe it is something that happened, the loss of a relationship that everyone thought would lead to something else. Or perhaps it is the loss of a job, the loss of a position of influence, or a public sin that brings public condemnation. Sometimes our opponents have found a way to triumph, perhaps by deceit.

In reality, this experience of rejection is often simply part of the primal rhythm of life, but at the time, the humiliation feels as though it has only happened to us. Everyone else seems to be doing so well. We pull into a cave in order to lick our wounds. Or we go out into some kind of wilderness, where there are few people, where no one will attack us, where things are a bit uncertain, and where we can sort things out.

For Moses, it was a crime that made him withdraw. He murdered someone, was found out, and he ran. If you were to come across him in the desert, as he took care of a few sheep, you might ask him why he didn't go back to Egypt, the place of his prestige and influence. With all his education and connections with the movers and shakers, why was he wasting his life? Why was he letting life just pass him by? Moses might have faltered, looked down, and kicked the sand with his grubby sandal. How could he have explained all that happened? And how could you have possibly understood? He was a criminal in his own land, a felon, so to speak. He was silent, hurting, and ashamed in the wilderness.

THE SNICKER OR THE LAUGH

Humiliation can be a killer.

The act of crucifixion in the ancient world was not designed to simply execute someone. It was not only designed to inflict the maximum amount of pain on someone, which it did. It was designed to humiliate. Despite the moving paintings we see, Jesus probably didn't even have a cloth wrapped around his midsection. He was stripped naked and pinned up for display, a sign above his head reading, "King of the Jews." Perhaps we can get the sense of the disrespect of the sign more easily by translating it as "Head Jew." The scene included mocking, blood, excrement down the crucified's legs, gasps from the victims, and laughter from the onlookers. I wonder which was the worst part for Jesus. On a human level, maybe it was the laughter. In T. S. Eliot's apt words—"I have seen the moment of my greatness flicker, I have seen the eternal footman hold my coat, and snicker"—maybe it was the snickering. He saved others, but He cannot save Himself.

I doubt the disciples were thinking of little golden crosses with jewels in them on a necklace when Jesus told them to take up their cross and follow Him. Rather, He was telling them, in a way, to embrace shame. He was telling them to uphold this dishonor, to honor it. Christians eventually turned things upside down. Later the world did not understand. How could this group possibly transform the ultimate sign of dishonor into their master badge of honor? For Christians to make the Cross their emblem may be the greatest inversion of all.

When one enters the wilderness, the normal trappings of a place in the community are taken away. One does not have the thousand little formalities that make us feel as though we are a part of society. Those little formalities help us pretend we are important. It could be a role in the family, a title at work, a place at the table with friends. In the wilderness, conveniences are removed, but more importantly, the affirmations we have been accustomed to get removed also. Often we get the opposite—disrespect and dishonor.

We still can't figure it out. Shame becomes a springboard for truth. The Christian scholar in the fourth century, Jerome, summarized this different kind of life, turning shame upside down, by describing the Christian life as to "nakedly follow the naked Christ." We follow without the clothing of honor we are used to. Our Master was disrobed too. We enter a different country when we enter this world.

It is the world of Sarah, where Hagar and others deride her for not having a child. She spent most of her life in the wilderness of unfruitfulness. It is the world of David, old and defeated, heading back to the desert in failure, betrayed by his son. It is the world of Winston Churchill, ridiculed by the same society he spent his life serving, although his heart fervently sought their affirmation. It is the world of Jesus. We can all recognize it.

It is the world of failure, which bears its own fruits that can turn the world inside out. It might be that there is accomplishment beyond the defeat. In that world, really, sometimes one fails in order to succeed. But when you are in the wilderness, you are not really sure there is another side to it. Maybe there is, maybe not. History teaches both lessons. This isn't an amusement park ride where you have the pretense of adventure but the security it will all be over in a few minutes when you will climb safely out of your little seat. There is real risk.

At the very least, one may look at things in the world of dishonor from a different angle—maybe it feels as though one is looking at things upside down. What is good may seem bad and what is bad may seem good. Commentator David Brooks makes this revealing comment in his book *The Road to Character*, a fitting paradox—"Success leads to the greatest failure, which is pride. Failure leads to the greatest success, which is humility and learning."

In certain circumstances, we learn humility through humiliation. Sometimes there may be a kind of cleansing when we are forced to embrace shame. Almost all of us spend part of our lives trying to live in the imagination of others, basing our lives on the approval of other people. Without admitting it, we often shape our actions and words to fit in with our own surroundings, whatever they are. Sometimes it is a particular person or a special group that really holds our report card in their hands.

An awful freedom can come when one is publicly dishonored. You realize in a different way that other people's viewpoints, whatever they are, do not really constitute who you are. A steely strength can grow beneath the dishonor. When triumph or public disaster comes, as the poet Rudyard Kipling said in his poem "If–," you can "treat those two imposters just the same." Shame doesn't have to rule you.

We can't come to the abundant side of dishonor too quickly. Maybe the story of Sarah points the way. Poor thing. In her context, having children was the ultimate standard of honor. But she was barren. It felt as though she was on the outside track, and life was just passing her by. She could probably hear the whispers of others as she walked along the road.

Hagar, her own servant, was fruitful when Sarah was not. Sarah felt she could even hear her own servant snicker. The indignity of it all. And worst of all, to have a husband whose name meant "father," and who was, shockingly, eventually given the name "father of nations." The humiliation, the questions, after he shared his name in a new place, the knowing looks that others exchanged about her. I can hear her now. *I'm completely barren, and now my husband's been given a name like that?* This barrenness didn't last for just a year or two. It lasted for decades—nearly her whole life, until hope was completely blanched from her weary heart. She was barren when she was young, and she was barren when she was old. The wasteland seemed to go on forever.

But maybe something happened in all that sterility. When Sarah finally heard the promise of God for a child, she didn't get all pious on us. She laughed. It was simply too unthinkable at her age. She had dealt with humiliation for so long she no longer seemed to care that it was so ridiculous. In the end, she seemed to even wear the absurdity of it all like a sign of honor.

We aren't told her inner psychology, but names were important in the ancient world, and we get a hint of how she responded to her situation by the name she gave her son, born so late in life—Isaac (Genesis 21:6). In Hebrew, Isaac sounds like the word for laugh. Let people laugh, Sarah seemed to say. I'm laughing too. His birth was a laugh.

She embraced the badge of absurdity. We can learn from her. What usually happens isn't what always happens. Unbelievable things happen all the time, and we have forgotten how to laugh.

WHEN YOU HAVE SHOT YOUR BEST FRIEND

Something else happens with dishonor—deep shame and guilt can ironically cleanse us of so much self-concern, and remind us of what is important. I remember hearing the story of George Truett, a great preacher in Texas in the late 1800s. He was well known and respected by nearly everyone.

One day, after he became pastor of First Baptist Church of Dallas, Truett was out hunting quail with one of his closest friends, the chief of police. In a freak accident, Truett shot his friend. Though they were able to get him to a doctor, his friend died.

After the incident, Truett struggled to return to the pulpit. It wasn't until Truett received what he believed to be a vision of Christ saying, "You are my man from now on," that he returned to his church to preach. On his return, other churches in the area cancelled their services so their members could hear him preach.

Public shame can be a turning point. Yet for some people, there is an even greater tragedy than this kind of shame. David paid a public price for his failure, but at least it was public—it seemed to matter. At least, we can suppose, when Sarah walked down the street, people talked about her failure to produce—they noticed her, anyway. Maybe Egyptian royalty snickered as Moses, the prince, returned to Egypt as a shepherd. But for some people, the greater hurt rests beyond the visibility of public antagonism.

Oddly enough, it is in one way the opposite shame—the shame of being invisible, not even being noticed. Where once you thought you were somebody, you realize you are a nothing, just an insignificant part of the landscape. No one recognizes your work. No one thanks you. No one is even aware of you. As we will see in the next chapter, you are simply a piece of furniture.

TAKEAWAY:

One of the hardest things about the wilderness is the shame.

Shame can be a springboard for a kind of freedom from approval.

Shame can simplify our hearts before God.

2

BECOMING A NOBODY

I am invisible, understand, simply because
people refuse to see me.

—Ralph Ellison, *Invisible Man*

*You've really made some smooth moves, haven't
you? Not only are you in jail. Not only are you
totally disconnected from your family. But you had
your little plan, didn't you? You thought you had a
way out of here. And you were right. You helped
out your fellow prisoner and explained his dream.
And all you asked was for him to remember you
when he got out. Just to put in a good word with
the ones who could get you out.*

*Now you've been waiting. First you were
eager. One day. Two days. A week. A month. Two
months. A year. On and on. Nothing. The realization slowly sinks in. He didn't hate you. He just
forgot you. You simply weren't important enough*

for him to even remember. You had such great goals when you started, but look at you now. You aren't a hero, and you're not a villain. You're just not important, a boring, fat zero, nonexistent. Now do you get it, Joseph?

JUST LOOK AT ME

This chapter is about being invisible. We started by talking about the fact that if you can't avoid the wilderness, then understand it. Then we looked at the heart of a lot of the wilderness—humiliation. But being unnoticed can be even worse.

Ralph Ellison wrote a powerful book about how it felt to be African American in the middle of the twentieth century. He called it *Invisible Man*. In the beginning of the book, the narrator tells a story of bumping into a tall, blond man in the dark. The man insults him, the narrator demands an apology, and he eventually throws the man down on the ground. Then the narrator comes to his senses. The blond man didn't really even see him. The blond man was being beaten up by an invisible man.

It is a terrible thing to feel invisible. Children know this. If they can't get attention for performing well, they will get attention for behaving badly. Being shouted at is better than not being recognized at all. And, as a children's worker at our mission sometimes says, "Some children are bigger than others." Some of us will still do anything just to get that attention.

As a person who has worked in the New York City with homeless people for more than thirty years, I see this kind of experience all the time. As the gap between the rich and the poor in our cities has accelerated, it becomes harder and harder to feel seen. People in the city get used to looking right through each other. Yes, it is unseemly that the homeless person smells bad, shouts obscene things, or sits in an obstructive place. But the worse feeling of all is to have another human being, dressed well and heading for work, refuse to even look at you. Being invisible can become toxic.

Then if you do need help in a large city, well, the bigger the city, the more depersonalized you can feel. It is difficult to have to wait all day only to face an overworked social worker or other service person who looks at you merely as an annoyance, a thing, a number obstructing their other more important work.

Sometimes I try to remember experiences in my own life when I had a small understanding of being treated that way. I became a Christian before my senior year of college, and all my plans changed. After graduating, I found myself roofing buildings, just to have a few dollars to survive. I especially remember one particular day when we were roofing part of the home of a very wealthy person. There I was, covered in tar and the dirt of the work, and the owner of the house came out. She was regal and efficient, walking across her manicured lawn. We, the grubby roofers, were a rather unfortunate necessity. She walked right past us. She refused to even acknowledge that we were there, much less thank us for what we were doing, or do something unthinkable, like offer us a glass of water.

I was young, and I was furious. I wanted to shout, "Hey! Don't judge me because my jeans are covered with tar. I am a human being too! Who do you think you are, anyway?" Being a nothing can feel even worse than being hated. Far worse.

BIG DREAMS DON'T MEAN A THING

Joseph's story is the prime example of being forgotten and ignored. He had prophetic dreams as a young man, and he probably told the wrong people at the wrong time. It probably wasn't the best idea to tell his brothers of his dreams of having dominion over his own family—even over his elder brothers. Those types of dreams could feed anyone's ambitions. But things didn't turn out the way he thought they would. First, he was betrayed by his brothers and sold as a slave. That's pretty bad. Anyone with a toxic family can understand that. I imagine he thought things couldn't get worse than that.

But they did. While serving as a slave, Joseph was falsely accused of rape, and the Egyptian accuser pulled the race card—Joseph was Hebrew—to win her argument. He found himself in prison and once again a long way from his dreams.

It wasn't long before Joseph saw an opportunity to better his situation. When he interpreted a dream of the pharaoh's cupbearer, who was also imprisoned, he asked to be remembered when the cupbearer was delivered, just as Joseph predicted. But when he was free, the cupbearer, "did not remember Joseph, but forgot him" (Genesis 40:23). Not even important enough to come to mind for two years—invisible.

It depends on the context, but issues of race, gender, poverty, incarceration, social standing—all kinds of things can make one invisible. Even age—the young can feel ignored as those who are older talk as though the young person is not even there, making decisions while ignoring those supposedly less experienced.

Where I grew up as a teenager in the Midwest, groups of men would sometimes refer to me as "son." It wasn't a kindly expression. To me, it said I was not quite able to be a part of the adults. I hated that word, "son"—I despised it. It made me feel nonexistent. I try to remember that feeling when someone else brings up such a word in their own context, and my first response might be, "What's the big deal?" The big deal, of course, is that for whatever reason, the word makes the other person feel like a nothing. And that matters.

WHEN DID I BECOME A HAS-BEEN?

Of course, growing older can do the same thing to a person. Winston Churchill had already experienced two wars and sat as a respected politician when he experienced his wilderness years. He had all kinds of talents and political connections most of us don't have. Youth can feel ignored, but something can sometimes happen when one ages. Once we were on the crest of the wave, riding the time with our particular skill. But suddenly, without warning, we become outdated has-beens. Our looks, our skills, our energy, our vocabulary become degraded. We don't hear as well, we don't remember as well, we don't look so sharp, we haven't seen the right TV shows. Unconsciously or not, we get excluded.

Where once we were in the mix, we become the person on the outskirts—or worse, politely patronized. Some people become more and more successful as they grow older. Others lose their jobs, their marriage, or their relevance, and they find to their surprise they are living a shadowy existence. It is a form of the wilderness. You are not admired or hated, merely tolerated—taken for granted, like an old chair.

Young or old, a lot of our feelings of being ignored have to do with our sense of identity. Moses was treated like a prince in Egypt. He had that identity. When he fled to the wilderness after killing an Egyptian, he became a shepherd. The Bible says shepherds were an abomination to the Egyptians (Genesis 46:34). From Moses's upbringing, shepherds were "low-lifes." So the journey to the wilderness was a challenge to identity for him. Was he Egyptian or Hebrew? Was he a prince or a shepherd? Was he a criminal or a potential liberator? It's sometimes hard to say you're a shepherd when you thought you were a prince. Or worst of all for some, you're a prince who has been completely forgotten. Life goes on without you.

Some of the people in the Bible head to the wilderness twice—once when they are young and then again when they are older. Hagar did, as did Moses and David. David faced devastating humiliation and returned to the desert as an older man. Certainly he was not invisible in one sense, as the deposed king, betrayed by his own son. On the other hand, in his internal world, as an aging man, he probably faced some of the process of feeling out of date and irrelevant.

Though a king, David found himself once again in the same place he once was as a young man—turned out, on the run, and heading for the desert. But this time the weight of his family failures weighed him down in a different way than when he was a young warrior. His own son had betrayed him. He was heartbroken, and yet he wished he could die for his son also. He wasn't sure he could stand up against an attack once again. It might be easier to see his entire life's work as a defeat.

We have the lyrics of some of David's songs during this time. Some scholars believe Psalm 63 was written about this second time in the desert. In these lyrics, David used his art and the context to funnel his grief. His parched, barren surroundings led him to cry of his thirst for God. It's funny how we sometimes feel the deepest closeness to God in our most difficult times. I wonder why—it is part of the secret of the wilderness. We only have the lyrics to David's song—I bet the music was haunting and probably perfect for the situation. "My soul thirsts for you," he sings (v. 1). "Your steadfast love is better than life" (v. 2).

We can't say for sure, but maybe David's experience in the wilderness as a young man, being a fugitive from the jealous King Saul, helped him to move his followers through the second time. Even his opponents commented that he was experienced in wilderness fighting. This is the kind of advantage that is hard to quantify at the time. Maybe we never can.

Perhaps aging is the ultimate wilderness. Jesus tells Peter after the Resurrection, "When you were young, you used to dress yourself and walk wherever you wanted, but when you are old, you will stretch out your hands, and another will dress you and carry you where you do not want to go" (John 21:18). Sometimes old age must feel like that, as people become less able to direct themselves. Shakespeare envisioned the last stage of aging that way—without teeth, without eyes, without taste, without everything. It is the wilderness of feeling like an object—an old appliance that is out of date.

THE ADVANTAGES OF BEING A NOBODY

Of course, when we feel like a nothing, we sense we are the only ones who have ever felt like that. Everyone else around us seems to have significance. We feel like the one lonely person at the party who's awkwardly picking at the chips alone, trying to act as though we have a purpose, while everyone else is talking away with friends and having a blast.

If we have no one who sympathizes with us, we still have a biblical support group—people in the Bible who had similar experiences. Paul is an example. No doubt he was gifted and called, but think of him at the end of his ministry, writing a letter to a younger man: "At my first defense no one came to stand by me, but all deserted me" (2 Timothy 4:16). He must have looked around to those he expected to receive support from, and said, "What am I, chopped liver?" The fact that you have had a long and fruitful ministry is not necessarily protection from feeling like a big zero, especially in times of need.

In Isaiah, the four servant songs—passages that anticipate the Messiah—touch on this quality of being a nobody. In one of the songs, the servant says he is not noticed—"he made me a polished arrow; in his quiver he hid me away" (Isaiah 49:2). The servant's experience is "hid," not appreciated or even perceived.

Next, the servant's work seems useless—"But I said, 'I have labored in vain; I have spent my strength for nothing and vanity'" (v. 4). The experience of looking at our own work and seeing it as useless and insignificant is something that affects us. In a later song, the servant is described as one who "had no form or majesty that we should look at him, and no beauty that we should desire him" (53:2). The fact of the matter is that this servant is simply not that impressive—once again, a piece of furniture.

Paul, when he reflected on Jesus, said that Jesus intentionally made Himself a nobody. Paul even used the language of nonexistence, of being a zero. Paul said Jesus was in the form of God, but "made himself *nothing* by taking the very nature of a servant" (Philippians 2:7 NIV, author's emphasis).

Are there any advantages to being a nothing? Are there advantages in having a non-identity, of being invisible? There might be. As we have said, the wilderness can be a place where your identity is questionable, and you get very little support. People who have gone through such a wilderness have said this to me in the past—"It made me evaluate my goals. Is my aim to get recognition for what I do? Or is my goal something else? Who am I really trying to impress anyway, and why?"

Being dishonored or ignored can change us. In an upside-down kind of way, having no recognition can strengthen your sense of self. It helps you realize your value doesn't live in other people's approval; your worth doesn't dwell in the imagination of others. When all the approval of others was withdrawn, you didn't cease to exist.

Even the world understands this. French philosopher Albert Camus said in his essay, "Return to Tipasa," "In the middle of winter I at last discovered that there was in me an invincible summer." In the midst of a silent, dreary winter on the outside, paradoxically, something else emerges within us.

If we have the misfortune (Or is it fortune?) of being a nobody in the wilderness, we can begin to think beyond ourselves differently. We can even begin to consider where value comes from. I recently heard a woman on the radio say, "God's love is not based on us; it's placed on us." Is my value really based on what I do, and who on earth recognizes it? Really? Isn't there something, or Someone, more?

There can be other advantages to being unrecognized too. You hear things you wouldn't otherwise hear. You can do good things in secret because no one is paying attention to you anyway. People can tend to underestimate you, and if you don't care who gets the credit, a lot can be accomplished. In writing about Saint Francis of Assisi, G. K. Chesterton implies that being a little fish can be better than being a big fish, because that little fish can pass through the net that is there to catch them.

Sometimes, a certain upside down joy can come if you don't expect or need the response of others. Chesterton continues as he talks about Francis:

> If a man saw the world upside down, with all the trees and towers hanging head downwards as in a pool, one effect would be to emphasize the idea of dependence. . . . He would be thankful to God for not dropping the whole cosmos like a vast crystal to be shattered into falling stars. Perhaps Saint Peter saw the world so, when he was crucified head downward. . . . In a . . . cynical sense . . . men have said "Blessed is he that expecteth nothing, for he shall not be disappointed."

It was in a wholly happy and enthusiastic sense that Saint Francis said, "Blessed is he who expecteth nothing, for he shall enjoy everything." It was by this deliberate idea of starting from zero . . . that Francis did come to enjoy even earthly things as few people have enjoyed them.

People sometimes sense a different kind of power in someone who is not getting noticed and doesn't care if he or she ever is. It makes one think. The other advantage is that when you have gone through the wilderness of being a nobody, you can see things that other people can't see. It is one of the perks of being underestimated.

AIMING LOW

I have told before the story of a man who helped me get started in ministry in the Lower East Side in New York City. It happened many years ago, but this is what I remember. He was blind and walked with a limp, yet he was refreshing to me somehow. Maybe it was because he didn't care. The area we lived in was full of abandoned buildings and had a high level of drug activity. This man and I were supposed to go on a church visitation together, two by two—an evangelistic ministry of our church. Honestly, I wished I had been assigned another partner.

We went to the building that was assigned to us. The intercom didn't work. We waited outside and talked, hoping someone would come in or out and let us in. Eventually someone did, begrudgingly. The journey to the third floor was a tough one. The stairway smelled like an unclean restroom. The second floor had a furious snarling German shepherd slightly restrained by a child's safety gate across one of the apartment doors. Somehow I got past the dog and wondered how I would ever get down.

Our discussion on the third floor was not particularly congenial. The person we were visiting was not impressed by me or my friend. The conversation grew louder and I got quieter. Finally the person we were talking to, thinking little of my partner, shouted, "You're nothing but a blind old man!"

My partner simply said with confidence, "I may be blind, but I can see more than you can." He was right. He had been through the wilderness.

Of course, Jesus gives some great party instructions when you are not being recognized or valued. He inverts our deep need to be seen and appreciated. He says, "Just aim low." When you are invited to a wedding, don't jockey to be at the front. Instead, "when you are invited, go and sit in the lowest place" (Luke 14:10). As He so often did, Jesus ended His instructions with one of those paradoxical zingers—"For everyone who exalts himself will be humbled, and he who humbles himself will be exalted" (v. 11).

Watchman Nee was a gifted Bible teacher and church planter in China. Following the Chinese Communist Revolution, Nee was persecuted and imprisoned and spent the last twenty years of his life in prison. He had a saying: "It is safest to put a cup on the floor." The implication was that if you, like a cup, choose the lowest place, you will not suffer the falls of those who reach higher. You won't get shattered. So invert your desires, he would say—just aim low.

Will Campbell was a Baptist preacher, writer, and prominent civil rights activist in the 1960s. He received a lot of hate mail from those angry at his civil rights stance. After developing quite the reputation as a civil rights activist, he realized he believed God hated all the same people he hated. He had to admit he had become little more than a "doctrinaire social activist," and that was different from being a follower of Jesus.

What changed him? I suppose his own wilderness. He recognized he had distorted the indiscriminate love of God for all people, without limitations. So he decided, of all things, to begin to spend time with members of the Ku Klux Klan. He befriended them. He spent time with them. He began to perform their funerals and weddings. When they were sick, he did tangible, practical things to help them, to clean up for them. Now he started getting hate mail from the other side of the political spectrum.

Once we are invisible for a while we realize we probably don't know the real causes for a lot of things about which we used to be so confident. We are certainly getting enough reports concerning the ones journalists think are shaping our world. But they may be wrong—we can't be so sure.

Thousands of years ago, a man who was supposed to be wise made this comment: "There was a little city with few men in it, and a great king came against it and besieged it, building great siegeworks against it. But there was found in it a poor, wise man, and he by his wisdom delivered the city. Yet no one remembered that poor man" (Ecclesiastes 9:14–15).

The wilderness can help you get to the point where it doesn't matter whether they remember you or not. If only things weren't so uncertain . . .

TAKEAWAY:

1. Part of being in the wilderness can mean becoming a nobody.

2. There are advantages to being "invisible."

3. If you are not being recognized, turn things around and aim low.

FINDING YOUR UNCERTAINTY

Can we actually "know" the universe? . . . it's hard enough finding your way around in Chinatown.

—Woody Allen

Now you've done it. You've alienated just about everyone—you must have, to be out here in the wilderness again. But this time you've got your child with you, and it's not just about you. You don't know where you are, do you? You just had to keep that secret mocking going, didn't you? Even your son picked it up. This is no joke. You have no map and no instructions, and you've run out of water. And it's getting hotter, Hagar.

Lost in the Fog and Thinking Stupid

One of the core implications of being in a wilderness is that you have no path. There is no road, no road signs, and no map. You don't really know where you are going. You're often lost. In the wilderness, you are frequently wondering which way to go. Everything feels so uncertain.

In the Bible, we know that the wilderness is often a real place. It is tangible. We are told that the woman Hagar, the mother of Ishmael, is sent out to the wilderness of Beer-sheba. The place is bleak and water is scarce. There might be a well somewhere, but she doesn't know where. It's the second time she has been ejected, excluded from her tribe. The Bible says she "wandered" (Genesis 21:14).

The sentences are terse describing what she does, but one can imagine, as the heat increases and her water gets less and less. It is her mother's heart for her son that weighs her down the most. When the water is gone, she finally hits a wall of despair. Hagar makes choices that only seem reasonable in her disoriented state. She leaves her child and goes some distance away because she doesn't want to watch her son die. It's that bad. She lifts up her voice and weeps (vv. 8–21). She is lost.

The wilderness or desert becomes the symbol for wandering in the Bible. The Old Testament scholar Walter Brueggemann put it this way—the wilderness is the "historical form of chaos." Uncertainty reigns.

In our own times, we talk about uncertainty and confusion a lot, but some fortunate people may not really know what it means to be literally lost. I was forced to remember this sensation about a year ago. I was hiking alone in the Appalachian Mountains, and the path I was on just petered out. It stopped in the middle of nowhere. I knew I needed to go to the top of the mountain, so I figured all I needed to do was keep heading up. I didn't need a path. It was January. I could see well enough. Bad decision.

In my mind, I started setting markers in the woods—a big stone, an odd tree—so that I could get back to the path if I needed to. Soon, the big stones and odd trees all started looking alike. I began to make little piles of rocks and stones every thirty yards, like Hansel and Gretel leaving bread, so that I could retreat to the path if necessary. Of course, I got to a place where I couldn't see my little piles of sticks anymore, and the woods started looking the same in every direction.

A fog rolled in, which made things even worse. The temperature dropped, and while I had been sweating before, struggling to get up the mountain, I began to think about hypothermia. The mind is funny when you are lost. There was no cell service, and I began to imagine how long it would take for my wife Susan to start worrying about me. I had told her where I was going, but I hadn't told her my more recent decision to leave the path.

As I tromped around in the woods, I eventually began to imagine my funeral. I saw it vividly in my head as I started to shiver. I hoped one of my acquaintances would give the eulogy. He was such a great speaker in those kinds of situations. Then I thought seriously about what would happen to my wife and how I would never see my children or grandchildren again. The fog got thicker, and the temperature kept dropping. I was really lost.

I wasn't really very far from civilization or safety. It just felt that way. I wasn't really lost for very long either. It just felt that way. I became thirsty and was breathing hard as I climbed. I knew this was no joke. I kept breaking through underbrush and piles of wood, which left scratches on my face, but I knew enough to head up the mountain. Finally, after what felt like decades, I ran into another trail. Nothing looked sweeter to me than that little brown path through the forest.

HOMELESS BUT NOT HOUSELESS

Let's face it. Being lost is no fun. It is much more fun to be confident and to know where you are going. Otherwise you may end up in a place where you are hungry or you are thirsty or you might die. Not everyone is foolish enough to get physically lost like I did. But almost everyone knows the feeling of being in a phase of life where the path is not clear, where we are uncertain of the next step. When we are in that kind of place, we feel alone, even though many others are in that same kind of uncertain place and are feeling alone too. And safety may be quite close—we just don't know it.

My life as a minister in New York City has included lots of lost people—not just lost as in I-don't-know-what-to-do-in-my-life lost but my-life-is-so-messed-up-that-if-someone-doesn't-help-me-I'm-going-to-die lost. Some of these people have been homeless, wandering like Hannah through the wilderness of the Lower East Side of Manhattan. If I am really honest, I find these kinds of people easier to work with than others. They know they need help, and they are not ashamed to admit it. And they don't care where the help comes from—a church, street person, God, the devil, a social worker, or anyone else. People who look like they have it all together can be just as needy, but working with them can be much more ambiguous for me, since they often don't acknowledge their needs.

I've also learned the truth of the statement penned by J. R. R. Tolkien: "Not all those who wander are lost." I remember a man who blessed our mission and neighborhood many years ago. He was intentionally homeless, choosing to live on the streets as a Christian to side with the poor. He helped us with the children and with giving out clothing in the winter. Since he himself lived on the street, his advice to those in need was very practical—stuff your clothing with newspapers to stay warm, and find a place out of the wind—things like that. I remember he used to say, "I am houseless but not homeless."

I suppose I see more people today who are the reverse of this man's statement. They are in some sense of the word homeless, but not houseless. They have a physical place to stay, but somehow, deep inside, they have lost their bearings, or perhaps they never had any bearings. No place is completely satisfying as they drift and wander from place to place, from work site to work site, even from church to church. Funny—even if we have a GPS, a map, and a place of our own, a sense of uncertainty can plague us. As a matter of fact, many who wander are lost, lost in the deepest sense of the word.

Is the Last Thing the Worst Thing?

Here's the point of this chapter. Being lost is not the end of the world. Being lost can be the end of the world. As a pastor, I have watched some people veer from circumstance to circumstance and then finally die, cut off from God and running from themselves. The wilderness holds real risk—it is not a game. Where I work, I feel as though we are in a battle. There are real victories, praise God, and there are real casualties.

In the Bible, lostness often precedes purpose. Our problem is we try to avoid the feeling of wandering altogether. We want to move from one phase of our life to another with no transition, uncertainty, grief, or wandering. We want to have the new marriage the day after the funeral, when in actuality we strongly need some in-between time.

The Bible is rich in lostness, uncertainty, and wandering. Abraham didn't become a superhero of the faith in a day, nor did Sarah, Hagar, Jacob, Joseph, or Moses—and on and on. The place of the wilderness matches our life.

Sometimes there is no clear path, and we usually don't know where things are headed no matter how confident we sound. It's just that we have never been there before. But in the Bible, the wilderness is not the end.

In the Book of Isaiah, the writer has an understanding of the devastating, and I mean totally devastating, time when God's people were exiled in Babylon. This period is another wilderness example. Their lives felt barren and arid while exiled. But God would eventually bring them through and out of exile. Likewise, after the Israelites left Egypt with Moses and wandered in the desert for forty years, they eventually came to something else—the Promised Land.

That doesn't mean that the roadless way in the wilderness is easy.

> When you pass through the waters, I will be with you; and through the rivers, they shall not overwhelm you; when you walk through fire you shall not be burned, and the flame shall not consume you.
>
> —Isaiah 43:2

Yes, in that uncertainty there are rivers and fire and flames. But there is also a promise.

James, the brother of Jesus, understood the wilderness in his own time, as he wrote to churches scattered abroad. He understood that in a sense they were separated from each other and from their true home. He called them the tribes in the Dispersion, a word that originally meant "scattered like seed." Then he spoke to those who didn't know what to do, "If any of you lacks wisdom, let him ask God" (James 1:5). Why? Because God is so generous (v. 5). When James talks about the wisdom God gives, one of the words he uses can mean that wisdom is without wavering or uncertainty (v. 17). For James, there is certainty on the other side of the need of those scattered.

Jesus understood the importance of how we look at things. He said the eye is the lamp of the body (Matthew 6:22). I have learned, in the work I do with people in the wilderness, to speak a certain way. We decide how we are going to look at things. When everything seems overwhelming, and I don't know what to do next, I have stopped crying, "What will I do? How can we proceed? I just don't know what to do!" Instead, I am learning to say, "We'll know." At the right time, we will know what to do. As overwhelming as the wilderness is, we will know what to do at the right time.

In the end, the wilderness feeling points to the heart of life. The heart of life is understanding that there is something on the other side. I remember reading many years ago about one woman who had been horribly abused as a child. She described her faith in this way as she proceeded to healing in herself: "I finally came to believe that there was something beyond the crucifixion, that as awful as Good Friday is, there is a Resurrection Sunday." That is the way the Christian writer Frederick Buechner described the resurrection—the resurrection means that the worst thing is not the last thing.

In the wilderness, I hold on to what I heard a traumatologist say in a training seminar to help us relate better with those in crisis. He worked mostly with people who had been diagnosed with terminal cancer, so he did not make the statement lightly. He said, "There is a hidden arrogance in despair, for despair presumes to know for sure that nothing good can ever come from this situation." How can we know for sure?

THE GOSPEL COMEDIAN IN OUR GROUP

Uncertainty in the wildernesses of life can have one other benefit. It punctures the false confidence some people hold on to, the kind of confidence of Job's friends, who presumed to know all the answers in the face of chaotic suffering. Might I say that a time in the wilderness will take the air out of my pomposity as I lecture my little thoughts to others? We can have a healthy assurance that God will make the best thing the last thing. We can also maintain an unhealthy presumption, assuming we know for sure what we don't know.

We have a person in one of our Bible studies who we call a gospel comedian. During this Bible study, those who are homeless or in transition can come together. Scripture says each should bring their gift to a gathering, so we ask him to bring a one-liner to make us laugh. We quote the Scripture passage that says to be not wise in your own eyes (Proverbs 3:7). Don't be too wise or speak too self-importantly. Each week our gospel comedian ministers to us—he gives us a one-liner to make us chuckle at ourselves. Human uncertainty can do a number of things, but one of the things it can do is make us laugh. We are all in this together, and the smartest of us all doesn't know much.

In a way, Bible teachers from the past are a support group for us when we don't know what to do. This week I read a book on the Reformation, which occurred five centuries ago, and I had such mixed feelings. On one hand, I rejoice in the joy people felt as they rediscovered reading the Bible for themselves, of seeing the wonder of grace, of returning to the simple truths. On the other hand, I was aware of the dark side of the Reformation and of those whose reformed beliefs put them in danger of being burned at the stake or otherwise killed for their beliefs.

In the middle of all this seriousness, I reread the introduction to a book written by Francois Rabelais, a scholar and a monk with a sense of humor. He wrote during the Reformation in the midst of all that serious debate. At the beginning of his most famous book, he wrote, "I'd rather write about laughing than crying, for laughter makes men human, and courageous."

If a challenge to our own false confidence can make us grin a bit, perhaps we can become more human—and even courageous—as we face the unknown regions of life. At least we can move to a place in the world where we stop strangling each other because of what we believe.

In a way, the time of uncertainty in our life can bring us back in balance. In the midst of trouble, we can find a deeper confidence in God's steadfast love for us. We can begin to see His invisible love through the totally inscrutable circumstances we face.

Yet the time of uncertainty can also guard us against a false confidence about God when we assume we know everything about Him and pontificate, like Job's friends, on the hows and whys of everything. The fifth-century theologian Augustine of Hippo put it this way: "God is not what you imagine or what you think you understand. If you understand you have failed."

What a strange way to look at it. But in the Bible, when Moses encounters God in the wilderness and asks for a name, God simply tells him, "I AM" (Exodus 3:14). To think you have a complete understanding of God means you have failed. In other words, realizing you have failed to totally understand God is a kind of success.

The wilderness can be the place of despair, the last gasp before annihilation. Yet it is not the last thing. Hagar, left in the wilderness, despairing over her child who is surely about to die, is at the end of her rope when she hears a voice asking a question. "What troubles you, Hagar? Fear not" (Genesis 21:17).

And here is what God did. He didn't change Hagar's circumstances. He didn't bring her water, create a water fountain, or anything like that. He simply "opened her eyes, and she saw a well of water" (v. 19). Apparently the water was already there; she just needed to be able to perceive it. Her son lived after all, and as God promised, he became the beginning of a great nation (vv. 20–21).

It's often the same for us. The help was right there. We just can't see it. Hagar couldn't see it. Nor could she really explain it. Her lostness preceded God's purpose.

TAKEAWAY:

1. Wilderness means not having a path.

2. Uncertainty is the badge of our time.

3. Lostness often precedes purpose.

4. In the Bible, the worst thing is not the last thing.

5. Uncertainty can puncture our false assurance.

4

SUBTRACTING RATHER THAN ADDING

Yes, our hopes are high, our plans colossal!
And we hitch our wagon to a star! . . .
We can move mountains, says St. Paul the great
apostle,
And yet: how heavy one cigar!

—Bertolt Brecht, *Mother Courage*

Well, what do you have left? All your friends deserted you. You are in jail. Winter is coming, and you don't even have a coat. You've always been so brilliant—everyone says so. Yet look at you. You have less than when you started out, and you didn't have much then. It's your friends' desertion that hurts the most, right when you needed them, at the trial. Is this the fruit of your entire ministry? So here you sit, in chains, alone, at the end of your life. What do you have left, Paul?

CHRISTIANS IN THE DESERT

We mentioned Paul before—old, in jail, deserted by those he depended on. He wanted his cloak, a few books, and parchments. He hoped Timothy would come before winter (2 Timothy 4:9–22). I wonder if he was tempted to hear the voice of accusation in his head. It's hard to read between the lines. Mostly, we hear the paradoxical note of joy in his letters from prison. How did that happen?

Meister Eckhart, a theologian born in 1260, said something that can turn our modern view of spiritual growth upside down. He said that God "is not found in the soul by adding anything, but by a process of subtraction."

Subtraction. Of course, we keep thinking that if we add this discipline or if we do that project, then certain virtues or blessings will be added to us. In some ways, our whole life can be an illusion—we add rooms to our houses and money to our mutual funds, and we think we are making progress. But in the journey of the heart, are we really making progress? We have forgotten the more important things happening may be the parts of our lives being taken away.

This is a chapter about loss. Going to the wilderness is almost always about loss—losing our role in life, losing our status, losing a loved one, losing our group of friends, losing our dreams, losing our superficial conception of ourselves, losing our previous understanding God. After the wilderness, things are rarely the same.

First we said that if you can't avoid the wilderness, then we must at least understand it. Then we talked about humiliation as part of the wilderness. Even worse sometimes, is being ignored or becoming invisible. Then we moved to the sense of confusion or lostness one can have in the wilderness. All these things involve loss. As if that is a necessarily bad thing.

In our mission, when we talk about recovery, we often refer to Jesus' words—"Seek first the kingdom of God and His righteousness, and all these things will be added to you" (Matthew 6:33). Added. That is the way we like to think. Put God first, and you get some additions. But as we read about the lives of people like Jesus and Paul, we see there is some subtraction going on too. As one grows older, some things become less and less possible. We usually see this as a bad thing, but as we read about the wilderness in the Bible, I am not so sure.

Some earlier Christians focused on the subtraction part. We don't have to agree with everything they said, but we can learn from them. The Desert Fathers and Mothers lived just a few hundred years after Christ, mostly in Egypt. They saw society's progressive approval of Christianity as a potential compromise. Political forces had approved Christianity, and it was consequently getting watered down. Probably people of wealth and power were starting to see becoming a Christian as a kind of "add on." In contrast, these committed men and women moved to the desert in Egypt, a sacrifice for their faith. They moved to the wilderness on purpose.

They saw the process of subtraction as a great blessing. They let go of their attachment to material things, for example. I used to have a story about the Desert Fathers in a frame on my wall at the office of the mission. Here it is as recorded in Charles Cummings's book, *Monastic Practices*:

> Two old men had lived together for many years and had never fought with one another. The first said to the other, "Let us also have a fight like other men do." The other replied, "I do not know how to fight." The first said

to him, "Look, I will put a brick between us, and I will say it is mine, and you say: 'No, it is mine,' and so the fight will begin." So they put a brick between them and the first said, "This brick is mine," and the other said, "No, it is mine," and the first responded, "If it is yours, take it and go"—so they gave it up without being able to find an occasion for argument.

Losing things in the wilderness was not necessarily seen as a bad thing. The idea of limiting oneself in the desert became a virtue rather than a liability. The wilderness wisdom encourages the process of letting go rather than adding, letting go of money, of irritable attitudes, of false self-importance.

Jesus said the same thing to His students: "So therefore, any one of you who does not renounce all that he has cannot be my disciple" (Luke 14:33). The one who is in the wilderness doesn't have to take himself or herself and everything else so seriously. The response of the student learning from the person in the desert was able to laugh when he was insulted—a great victory.

THE GREATEST THING ABOUT LOSING IT ALL

Years ago, there was a person on the street who came to the mission who knew he had mental health problems, though I don't know what the professional diagnosis would have been. He had all kinds of strange views, politically and otherwise, that kept him on the fringe and sometimes in trouble with the law. However, he was endearing. He knew he had problems, but he refused to let those problems destroy him. I remember him once proclaiming with great joy concerning his own mental capacity, "The greatest thing about losing it all is that you don't have to carry it with you."

Too true. For all of us.

At seminary, one of my professors told me of a friend who treasured her house and the beautiful family heirlooms it contained—exquisite old silver and china carefully on display in beautifully appropriate cabinets. One night this woman's house burned down completely. She confessed to the professor of a shocking feeling as the house went up in flames—relief. She didn't have to hold onto, protect, explain, or develop all those things anymore. The loss of those things did the opposite of what she expected. The subtraction she experienced somehow became an inner enlargement.

People who have been in the wilderness know that the more we lose, strangely enough, the more we appreciate what we have. In the middle of the nineteenth century, Russian writer Fyodor Dostoevsky was sentenced to execution by the authorities for his political stance. At the last moment, as he and his fellow prisoners were preparing to be killed, the execution was stayed. While in prison, Dostoevsky was only permitted to read his New Testament Bible. Dostoevsky's faith intensified. He wrote about the firing squad experience in his novel, *The Idiot*, twenty years later. This was his thought process: As he waited for the firing squad, he knew he had minutes left to live. Each minute of life became extremely precious. He thought what an eternity of life he could live if he weren't shot.

Moses lost his birth family, adopted family, and prestige when he went to the wilderness the first time. Hagar lost family and nearly the life of her son when she was sent to the wilderness. David lost his family, his job, and his place in the community as he was chased into the wilderness the first time. Somehow each had deeper experiences with God in that time of subtraction. We might say such a perception is obvious as we read about someone else. It is harder to accept when we are sent into the deserted place ourselves—loss can hurt so much.

Is It Giving Up or Is It Letting Go?

Working with people who often find themselves without homes, family, resources, or prestige, I have heard this statement more than once: "I kept saying that Jesus was all I need, but I really didn't know it until He was all I had." Subtraction.

This brings us to grief—that deep sorrow over affliction or loss. Most of the time, grief is part of the journey into the wilderness. Loss often precipitates the journey to the desert. One of my best friends was a hospice chaplain. After spending years listening and helping people who were facing death, he said, "Facing death is really not about giving up. It is about letting go. It is accepting that I won't see my grandkids, I won't take that trip, I won't write that book, I won't climb that mountain." My friend eventually received a diagnosis that indicated he too would die soon. He died profoundly.

The experience of subtraction can break our heart. Aging can be a wilderness experience in itself. A young person naturally holds all these dreams about what he or she will accomplish. It is how we survive. Slowly, as life progresses, we see that some of those things will never happen, the possibilities of youth become less and less. As the German playwright, Bertolt Brecht, expressed it, our plans are colossal, but we find that even lifting something as small as a cigar takes a lot more than we expected.

The spirit of our own time has taught us we cannot run from grief. Previous generations advocated cultivating a stiff upper lip. Now we call that approach "denial." In other words, if we repress grief, or deny it, then grief doesn't really go away. It will return in a more destructive mode, demanding a sacrifice from our health, our relationships, or our very being.

Going to the wilderness often means facing our grief—identifying what our grief really is. The Bible doesn't deny this experience. In the Book of Ruth, Naomi has two sons, and they both die. She is left destitute in a foreign land. When she returns to her homeland, she tells the others not to call her Naomi any more, but she gives herself a new name—the word that sounds like "bitter"—and says, "I went away full, but the Lord has brought me back empty" (Ruth 1:21). Subtraction. Of course we know her hard-nosed assessment of the situation is realistic for the time, but in the end, things are not bitter for her, though her loss is still there. Once again in the stories in the Bible, we see the wilderness doesn't always last forever.

Few people outside of the faith community use the word *idolatry* anymore, unless it is transformed into something positive, like a singer who becomes America's "idol." However, in the Bible, this word contains one of the deepest truths in life. Not many things last forever. Not people, things, or places. Not forever. The people and things we hold dearest will eventually pass away, or we will pass on before them. In a sense, idolatry is trying to hold on to something or someone perpetually, which just isn't possible. One of my main jobs as a pastor is to help people come to terms with this understanding. I love to go to the hospital to pray with a young couple when they have their first baby. I don't enjoy doing funerals in the same way, for old people or for young people, but it is an inevitable part of life also.

In the end, loss helps us understand what our true goals are. For example, if I am grieving because I didn't get recognition after years of service—well, was the recognition the reason I did the work? Or if one important person criticized what I did in the work—well, was I doing the service for that person's affirmation? If I lose a friend to a disease—well, is the quality of my life determined only by the existence of that friend? Is the quantity of years the only way to measure value in life? That process of subtraction in living helps us know what is ultimately important.

Going into the desert simply clarifies the fact that we are choosing things in life and when we do, we lose things too. There is no selection without rejection.

CURSES AT A FUNERAL

A man our church has known for many years in our neighborhood was very close to his mother. When she died, he was heartbroken. He felt lost and descended into a wilderness of grief. He chose to medicate himself in order to get rid of the pain. He paid a price. Months later, he was found dead on his sofa, surrounded by bottles of alcohol.

The memorial service was a tough one. What can you say? We remembered the good things in his life. One of his sisters was honest enough to say how angry she was with him, but also how much she loved him. Many of the people this young man grew up with were drug dealers who had an impact on others in the community as well. One man got up and said, "Let's just get this straight. We've all messed up in this room. One of our buddies has died. Some of us are still messing up. But some of us have left this junk. I did two years ago, and I am glad. We can't bring my buddy back, but we have today. We can let this bad thing be a good thing. We can choose today."

His point was clear and true, and the people in the room listened to him in a way that they would never listen to me.

A loss helps us decide what is important and what is not. When we go into the wilderness, we lose things. We lose our way, we lose our status, we lose or sense of self, we lose the normal ways we function. When we lose things, we have to make choices about what is going to keep us going.

ATTITUDE OR SKILLS?

Paul understood that we could change in how we view things. He had it all figured out when he was younger and knew exactly what to do—persecute Christians. And he must have been pretty good at it too. But on his way to arresting some more Christians, he saw a flash of light and fell to the ground. There on the ground, when he asked whom he was addressing, he got the reply, "I am Jesus, whom you are persecuting" (Acts 9:5). I imagine this was the last thing Paul expected, given his worldview. Due to his own vindictive activities, he probably found it particularly horrifying.

But then, Jesus said something to Paul that I think he never quite got over. Jesus said, in effect, I want you on my side (vv. 1–18). Where did Paul go after all this happened? Where else? To the desert of Arabia (Galatians 1:17).

Paul was not unacquainted with the wilderness. He went to the desert of Arabia presumably to sort out his encounter with Christ. In reflecting on his experience, Paul used the language of loss and subtraction.

By the time he wrote Philippians, he was in jail. He was facing his own death, but he made a choice. He did not allow his impending execution to have its desired effect—to make him fearful or retract his goal. Instead, Paul chose to frame the execution as a win-win scenario: "For to me to live is Christ, and to die is gain" (Philippians 1:21). After adding up all the things he had accomplished before he was a Christian, he said, "Indeed, I count everything as loss because of the surpassing worth of knowing Christ Jesus my Lord. For his sake I have suffered the loss of all things and count them as rubbish, in order that I may win Christ" (3:8).

Paul makes it clear. First, he lost it all—all those things he thought were so great and important before. Second, he saw that such loss is worth it in order to achieve his new goal, to gain Christ.

Paul had been to the desert, reflected on these things, and reframed his priorities. He involved himself in what was sort of a grand reconsideration of his own experience. Going to the wilderness, experiencing loss, can often help us make reconsiderations of cosmic proportions. It happened for Paul.

Reconsidering priorities means choosing how you are going to see them. Paul is very aware of this. He instructs the Philippians to make a choice in terms of what they think about. He tells them to think about what is true, honorable, just, pure, and lovely (4:8).

One of the fruits of being in a wilderness, whether literally in the wild, or in an inner state of desert, is we see once again that we make choices—choices in how we handle the wilderness.

Many years ago I went to a survival course for a week, learning skills such as using mud as camouflage for hunting, starting a fire without a match, and making a knife out of stone. Unfortunately, I no longer remember many of the skills I was taught. But one thing stayed with me. The head instructor told us that when you are in a survival situation in the wild, you need two things—survival skills and a survival attitude. He said that of the two, survival attitude was more important.

When we are in the wilderness, we learn once again that what we choose can determine what happens. We can choose some things that will lead to life, and we can choose some things that will kill us.

We know this on an earthly level. I think of the story of the little boy that goes outside with a baseball bat and a ball, and says, "I am the greatest batter in the world." He throws the ball up, takes a swing at it, and misses. He does it again, "I am the greatest batter in the world." He misses again. He does it again and misses.

The next time the boy throws the ball in the air, he says, "I am the greatest pitcher in the world." We all make choices in how we see things.

Here is a phrase from Paul that has helped me through a thousand little wildernesses. Paul says, in effect, that love does not rejoice in what is wrong but rejoices in what is right (1 Corinthians 13:6). At work, in marriage, in family, in examining our own lives—we can choose to rejoice in what is wrong or spend time rejoicing in what is right.

BE SECRET AND EXULT

Losing things, experiencing subtraction, forces us to reexamine and sometimes reframe. William Butler Yeats wrote a poem concerning the wilderness of loss. He titled it, "To a Friend Whose Work Has Come to Nothing." There's a wilderness title for you. Sarah, Moses, Hagar, and David, could understand that title. Yet Yeats helps us understand how loss and futility can help us see the world differently. The last part of the poem goes like this:

> Bred to a harder thing,
> Than Triumph, turn away,
> And like a laughing string,
> Whereon mad fingers play,
> Amid a place of stone,
> Be secret and exult,
> Because of all things known,
> That is most difficult.

Yeats helps us see we can view failure in a completely different way. Loss can, paradoxically, result in exulting.

Think about Joseph, our poster child of subtraction. Beloved by his father? Subtraction: sold into slavery. Part of a close family? Subtraction: betrayed by his brothers. High level of honor? Subtraction: made into a slave. Honor as a slave? Subtraction: falsely accused and sent to prison. Remembered for his kind help of a fellow prisoner? Subtraction: forgotten by that prisoner for two years.

When his fortunes are finally turned around, what were his inner thoughts like? The Bible doesn't use psychological words in the way we do. However, we know that in the ancient world, names were important. They give insight into the character of a person or their parent.

Joseph has two sons. He could have named one "It's not fair what happened to me" and the other one "Someday I will pay my brothers back." Instead, he gives one a name that sounds like "making to forget" because Joseph said, "God has made me forget all my hardship" (Genesis 41:51). The other son he gave the name that sounds like "making fruitful" because Joseph said, "God has made me fruitful in the land of my affliction" (v. 52).

In other words, after all his loss, Joseph chose to see the good that came from it. Of course, by the time he had children, he was on the other side of the wilderness of subtraction. Perhaps, if he'd had to name children while he was in prison, he might have named them "Get me out of here!" and "Send me a cake with a file in it!"

David had a similar experience as a young man. Beloved by his king? Subtraction: the king tries to kill him. Honored by the people? Subtraction: troops aiming to capture and kill him. Close to his family? Subtraction: has to run to another country. Filled with a sense of honor and heroism? Subtraction: has to act as though he is crazy in order to survive. Lived in a palace? Subtraction: living in a cave (1 Samuel 21:10—22:2).

Yet when David writes a song about the experience, he does not start it as a lament. He chooses to focus on the fact that he is alive. He starts out by saying, "I will bless the LORD at all times; his praise shall continually be in my mouth" (Psalm 34:1).

We all know this truth intuitively. Ironically, sometimes the more we lose, the more we see we have, and sometimes the more grateful we become. But we may have to make a choice on how we see it.

I have lived my adult life working in a mission with people who have often been ground down, homeless, heroin addicts, alcoholics, and mentally ill. I see change can come when they believe what God says about them, when they choose to see life differently.

One such man shared how he had mental health issues, and he woke up every morning filled with fear and anxiety. He knew what it was like to be in a strait jacket. He knew mental health institutions, homeless shelters, and the street. He said it took him a great amount of courage just to get out of bed. But he was gripped by the promise that he was a new creature in Christ. He chose to laugh at his difficulties.

He shared with me things he said to himself every morning. "I refuse to fear. I have already won the victory. I am not a victim but a victor." In some ways, this man had lost so much in life. He owned very little. He didn't even have the natural ability to get out of bed in the morning without high anxiety. Lots of subtraction. Yet somehow, by his choices, he influenced those around him who had been crushed—far more than anyone else could have influenced them. Those professionals who had added degrees and position and money to their lives seemed paltry in comparison.

TAKEAWAY:

1. The wilderness teaches us the advantages of letting go rather than adding on.

2. Paradoxically, the more we lose, the more we appreciate.

3. Grief is that journey of seeing that we can't idolize any person, place, or thing in this world.

4. Loss helps us reframe our lives.

5

GIVING UP INSTEAD OF GIVING IN

Everything I've ever let go of has claw marks on it.

—David Foster Wallace

How long will you wait? You've seen most of your friends die off. You came close to the Promised Land, and then you watched it recede as you spent another forty years wandering in the wilderness. You were so close, but now you've grown older—sixty, seventy, eighty. It would have been so easy through the years to tell the people, "I told you so." Time to keep your mouth shut, Caleb.

DID JESUS JUST CALL HER A DOG?

The last chapter was about subtraction and loss. This chapter is about the other side of letting go. You can let go of a dream without giving in. Caleb had a dream of entering the Promised Land as a relatively young man. Yet, he didn't get to enter as that younger man.

When Caleb was chosen as one of the twelve spies to scope out the Promised Land, he had to give a minority report. The other spies said, "We can't," but Caleb and Joshua said, "We can." The other spies saw the inhabitants as giants in the land and themselves as grasshoppers in comparison. Their assessment of the challenge was inflated, and they paid a price for their refusal to trust. Caleb had to go back into the wilderness with them for another forty years. He paid a high price and had to give up part of his dream, and one could say it really wasn't his fault (Numbers 14:30). Caleb gave up years and years of his life, but he didn't give in.

My own mother would tell the story of having five young children and finding herself in the hospital. In many ways she hated her life. While in the hospital, she said a prayer, and the essence of it was something like this: "OK, Lord. I give up. My life is Yours. Do with me what You wish."

According to her testimony, this is when her life began to change. She won by giving up. When I was a young man and trying to sort things out, I asked her to tell me her story more than once.

Others tell stories of healings—of praying and praying and getting no result and of finally saying something like this: "OK, Lord, I give up. I want You more than I want a bodily healing. Whatever happens, I yield myself to You." Sometimes, ironically, things begin to sort themselves out in our bodies when we let go of the insistence that things get sorted out.

Sometimes the wilderness will remove our dreams. We experience loss and grief. But we don't have to lose our grit. In fact, the wilderness time can give us a different kind of grit, something stronger.

Do you remember that story where Jesus calls a woman a dog? With modern spectacles on, this is a tough story. This woman had to give up her dignity to cry out to Jesus on behalf of her oppressed daughter—she couldn't quietly ask. At first Jesus didn't answer her. But the woman didn't give in. The disciples found her a bother. They asked Jesus to send her away. The woman had to give up hope for an easy answer. She probably had to give up her dream for Jesus to simply turn to her and respond. But she didn't give in. Then Jesus answered, "I was sent only to the lost sheep of the house of Israel" (Matthew 15:24). Jesus spoke of His calling in this phase of His ministry, but for this woman who is not an Israelite, this response must have been a stunner.

But this isn't the end of the story. The woman gave up her vision of propriety and knelt before Jesus. She boiled it down to the basics. "Lord, help me" (v. 25).

Another rebuff came, "It is not right to take the children's bread and throw it to the dogs" (v. 26).

OK. Time to quit. Time to say, "He hurt my feelings. I can't believe He just said that. I am never going to church again. I'll show them." But the woman doesn't do that. She doesn't give in. She came back with a smart answer. "Yes, Lord, yet even the dogs eat the crumbs that fall from their master's table" (v. 27).

I like to think Jesus smiled at this point. He was testing her, prodding her, pushing things to the limit. Why are situations often like that, even in the spiritual world? Why does Jacob have to wrestle with God and finally say, "I will not let you go unless you bless me" (see Genesis 32:26)? Why do we so often have to meet resistance after resistance after resistance and give up our last shreds of our little vision of how it is supposed to happen before we see something happen? Why do we have to give up without giving in?

I think God likes to see a little grit in us, don't you? A little pluckiness, a refusal to give in. If we love our children, we want to see that virtue grow in them, that steadfastness, that refusal to let some small-scale speed bumps make us quit. So Jesus smiled, I think, and said, "O woman, great is your faith! Be it done for you as you desire" (Matthew 15:28). And the Bible says the woman's daughter was healed instantly.

Challenges in the Morning of Life

Perhaps our whole journey of life is learning how to give up the things we expected without giving in to despair. The wilderness can prune away many of our anticipated dreams, and Jesus said that the Father (often referred to as a gardener) will prune us. Of course, this kind of pruning has a purpose. There is another side to the wilderness— fruitfulness (John 15:1–2).

I don't know why we so often come to truth through opposites. Jesus certainly understood that. I don't know why the other side of diminishment is expansion. We see this truth all the time, in the world and in ourselves. Pierre Teilhard de Chardin, a scientist and Catholic priest, wrote a meditation to God called *Hymn of the Universe*. In it he included this prayer: "Bring me to a serene acceptance of that final phase of communion with you in which I shall attain to possession of you by diminishing within you." Diminishment and possession—this process of the soul.

It is hard to let go of things. As David Foster Wallace said, we often leave claw marks on what we mean to let go of.

It is time to talk a bit more about aging. Psychiatrist Carl Jung made a comment that is helpful to me. He said that life has a morning and an afternoon. Each half has its seasons and its particular challenges.

I'll start with some of the challenges of the morning of life, or the first half of life. First, we face the wilderness of realizing that life isn't turning out the way we thought it would. Perhaps this is not a universal realization. Perhaps there are people for whom life has come about just as they expected, but I have not had the privilege of talking to them much. I listen more to people who are grieving the loss of their hopes.

One person grieves because they see their career possibilities diminish. Another person faces the insecurity that they have not found that special one to be their companion. Another longs for a child and can't understand why God hasn't given them one. On the other hand, another person has children and asks, is this all there is? Another person faces the bewilderment of achieving their professional goals, but finds his or her life empty of personal value other than what comes from their résumé.

This is the journey of diminishment that can characterize the morning of life. In the nineteenth century, Thomas Cole painted four paintings called *The Voyage of Life*. In the first picture, a child is in a boat in a fresh green landscape of flowers, and an angel is guiding the boat with the rudder.

In the second painting, a young man has confidently taken charge of the rudder of the boat, and he is leaning forward in hope, heading toward a beautiful palace in the air. He has left the angel on the shore. The trees and hills around the river are green and full.

But the third painting is filled with rocks and waves and a storm. The boat is damaged and the tiller, which guides the boat, is gone. The palace is nowhere to be seen. The angel is far away and the sky is filled with darkness. The man has lost control. Evil spirits loom in the clouds. The boat is headed for a crash, and the man is looking upward, helpless in the craft, praying.

This is what can happen later in the morning of life. At some point, the clear skies vanish. The young person doesn't feel in charge any more. In fact, the tiller is broken off. The beautiful palace, that loomed so large on the earlier canvas, is no longer in sight. He hasn't yet made it to the fourth painting—a painting where the water has calmed.

Let's be honest. Cole's third painting is a picture of the wilderness of life. No tiller, little control, a vanished hope, rocks and destruction ahead. One of the choices in the wilderness in the morning of life is to give up and give in.

My work at the mission often feels like a battle. There are great victories and also casualties. Some of the people I work with seem bent on destruction. Any hope of a castle is gone. All they see are rocks ahead. Some destroy themselves quickly and some more slowly. I've performed way too many funerals and memorials for young people.

But I am not just talking about those who are in difficult circumstances. Fame and success are no protection from self-destruction. Youth itself is no protection. One hopes the list of the "27 Club" gets no longer, but it probably will. Jimi Hendrix, Janis Joplin, Jim Morrison, Kurt Cobain, Amy Winehouse—all famous musicians who died at the age of twenty-seven, each with their own sad story of self-destruction and talent lost so early.

WHY DO I HAVE TO GO THROUGH THIS AGAIN?

In the first half of life, what is the reason for that feeling that life has not turned out as you have planned, that you are out of control in the midst of a dreary storm? As we have said, in many ways, diminishment can lead to destruction, or it can lead to expansion. Sometimes a young person can act as a hero and triumph over the wilderness. Sometimes a person can survive the pathless territory yet see no purpose in doing so. But one of the long-term reasons to survive the wilderness is so you can help others get through it too.

Jung and other psychiatrists in his school are probably right. We can't live the afternoon of life with the program of the morning of life. Trying to live the afternoon of life with the same values and goals of the morning time might become in the end a way of living a lie. Part of the challenge of the afternoon of life is to find ways to help those who are in the morning of life.

Psychologist Erik Erikson talked about a later stage in life when we make the choice between generativity and stagnation. As we age, we must find ways to be giving and productive, to nurture things that will outlast us. Otherwise, we become more self-absorbed and more and more stale.

In the classic sense of going into the wilderness or the desert, some of the Bible characters are sent into the desert twice. Hagar is sent into the desert before her baby is born and then again when she wanders but also has to care for her child. Moses flees to the desert alone after his act of murder and stays for forty years. Then he returns to the desert followed by a nation. His familiarity with the wilderness could not help but be an asset.

David flees from Saul to the wilderness in the morning of his life but must go again in the afternoon of his life when his own son betrays him and drives him out. In the second time, he leads the shadow kingdom, those who are faithful to him as king. The fact that he is an experienced warrior in the wilderness is even noted. Often when someone goes into the wilderness a second time, more depends on the journey because more people are dependent on the person. The second time, the person can be more helpful, I suppose, because he or she is not a stranger to the desert.

Perhaps this helpfulness is one of the things an older person can bring to a younger person, if the older person is not a stranger to the desert. If one finds no other reason for the wilderness, perhaps the reason for the first wandering is so the person can help others survive through it later.

The challenge of the wilderness in the morning of life is to find meaning and purpose for what we are doing. In the biblical story line, the people who wander often experience God in a deeper and truer way. Perhaps the challenge of the wilderness in the second half of life is to find ways to help others and care for others in the inevitable wilderness time.

HOW TO BE AN OLD CRONE

Senex is a Latin term for "old man." It is often used today for a man or a woman. As Carl Jung and others thought about aging, they began to use this term for the wise old man (or woman) who often appears in stories of adventure and the development of a hero. In stories, a *senex* often appears and helps the hero move to the next phase.

Merlin was a *senex* for King Arthur. Gandalf was a *senex* for Bilbo and Frodo in *The Hobbit* and The Lord of the Rings series. Professor Digory Kirke becomes a sort of *senex* for the children in The Chronicles of Narnia. Modern culture has them everywhere: Albus Dumbledore in the Harry Potter series, Mr. Miyagi from *The Karate Kid*, Yoda in the Star Wars franchise, Professor X in The X-Men comics, Nick Fury in The Avengers comics, and so on. The older figure appears in a time of need and helps the younger man or woman encounter the perplexing challenge (wilderness) that is faced.

My favorite *senex* is Gandalf—old, with a sense of humor and a care for the little hobbits and others. He is in the battle, but his larger goal seems to be helping the others as they encounter the dark wood, a perplexing mountain world, or Mordor. Bilbo is not the same person at the beginning of the story that he is at the end. Neither is Frodo or Samwise. In the story, Gandalf has to face his own "dark night of the soul" in battling the horrible Balrog. One feels as though it is not his first major struggle.

How much did Isaac learn from Abraham or Timothy from Paul—people who had gone through the wilderness and were able to encourage the next generation? It is essential.

Caleb had to give up his dream of entering the Promised Land as a younger man. He had to wait for forty-five years. How encouraging was it when he was later able to stand up and say, "I am this day eighty-five years old. I am still as strong today as I was in the day that Moses sent me" (Joshua 14:10–11)? Then he asked to take the hill country, where the giants lived. His hope was deferred but not canceled. He still had adventures ahead of him, even if the experience would be different from his earlier days. I hope the younger people there listened carefully.

The wise woman is one kind of *senex*. Some people today are trying to recover the positive meaning for *crone*. They say the word origin could come from time (*chronos*), meaning crones are long lasting. They have survived. How hard it is for us to recover the wise older woman in our culture? Stories abound concerning a good fairy godmother who helps a person like Cinderella. But in movies, wise women often have to be old and young at the same time, like Mary Poppins, or the Good Witch in *The Wizard of Oz*. Still, things are changing. We've enjoyed more characters like Maggie Smith's wise and perceptive Dowager Countess in *Downton Abbey*.

Mother Teresa is one who could be seen as a *senex*, a crone in the best sense of the word. She, with her heart for others, has lasted beyond death, as a wise spiritual leader. Julian of Norwich was a woman who lived into her seventies and shared her experiences of Christ in writing. The value of the older woman is being recovered in the "Titus 2" women's movement. Women adopt the Scripture (Titus 2:3–5), where older women are to teach and train younger women.

Women in the Bible have gone to the wilderness. How much could one learn about waiting from Sarah or about earning respect in a man's world from Deborah or about being a teacher and mentor in a new movement of God from Priscilla?

So here is the point of all this—if you feel you have passed your prime and are no longer the hero of the story—then why not be a *senex*? Be a Gandalf or a good godmother. Help the younger ones have an adventure. You don't have to have the adventure in the same way you did in the morning of life. But you have something to give—if only your experience in the wilderness. Turn things upside down in our youth-dominated culture. Recover the value of being an old man or a crone. Trying to relive the adventure of the morning of life only shows arrested development. But an attitude of helping the younger will bring you back into the adventure in a new way.

And, if you are a young person, then cultivate mentors. You will need the Yodas and the Professor Xes and the Dowager Countesses as you encounter the pathless regions before you. You ignore them at your hazard. Become a hero in your wilderness, not a zero without guides.

WHICH WAY WILL YOU TURN IN THE WILDERNESS?

The wilderness can take a dark turn. In the early stages of life, one can follow the destructive trajectory of the 27 Club. But the older person can take a dark trajectory too. The old man can become the bitter old man, angry at the world and God for all the loss and hardship in the world. The old woman can become the hag, needy and destructive and fearful.

Let me share some thoughts about the writer Ernest Hemingway. The thoughts will say more about me than about him. I don't presume to know his inner journey, the heartache, and tragedy of the end of his life.

As a young man, there was a phase when I wanted to be just like Ernest Hemingway. He had adventures. I wanted adventures. He didn't believe in God. I didn't believe in God. He went to Europe. I went to Europe. He took up boxing. I took up boxing. He wore a moustache. I tried to wear a moustache (except I looked like a sixteen-year-old version of Hitler). He wrote a lot as a young man. Well, I dabbled in writing, just a little, like in my journal . . . sometimes. He appreciated the tangible things in life. I wanted to appreciate the tangible things in life.

I had my own journey in the wilderness, groping and lonely for a year in Berlin, wondering if there was anything more to life than what I saw around me. I was provided with a junior year abroad. At first, I was very lonely. I didn't believe in God and was convinced everything around me was the result of time plus space plus chance. One night, alone in my room in Berlin as a twenty-year-old, I said a prayer in anger, a rebellious word. I said, "God, if You are there, why don't You just show Yourself?"

I sat there, and I didn't see or hear anything. But I felt a presence, which seemed to come from the top of the room, another center of consciousness that was there in the room with me. The presence was kind, gracious, generous, and benevolent. My response was not happiness. It was fear. I began to perspire. I didn't want that presence at all, and slowly the presence began to withdraw. I felt as though the presence was saying, "You summoned Me, but I will not force Myself on you."

My experiences in that wilderness, lonely as it was, made me tender later on to the work of God, and I eventually became a Christian. After becoming a Christian, I still admired Ernest Hemingway, but I began to read about him in a different way. I remember reading a letter he wrote when he turned fifty, when he was so proud that on his birthday he wrote 573 words before breakfast, made love multiple times, drank a case of champagne with friends, and went fishing. It seemed to me, even as a young man, that his development had been arrested, as if he was still trying to prove himself and live the morning program when he was entering the afternoon program.

Apparently the time in his fifties was a tough time. He entered a different kind of wilderness from all the adventures he had before. At times, he felt his writing skills were diminished, and he was experiencing rapidly declining health. For a variety of reasons, his mental health deteriorated. His family had a history of committing suicide. Eventually, at the age of sixty-one, he killed himself with a shotgun. After I became a Christian, I wanted to look at life in a different way, and Hemingway's journey was not so attractive after all.

A wilderness holds real risk. The trajectory of a person can go so many different ways. For Winston Churchill, the wilderness didn't last a month or two for him—it lasted ten years. During his wilderness years, he was nearly broke, had become increasingly out-of-date, and was considered a has-been. He had to deal with depression.

But at age sixty-five, after World War II started, Churchill became prime minister. All the great speeches we hear from Churchill, most of the inspiring phrases that still grip us come from the time after his wilderness years—"finest hour," "blood, toil, tears, and sweat," "never . . . was so much owed . . . to so few," and so on. Even for an older person, there can be new adventures beyond the wilderness. Churchill coped in his own way.

Churchill embodied the idea that success is the ability to go from failure to failure without losing your enthusiasm. He kept on going. True, even in the first part of World War II, Churchill encountered failure after failure. But I believe his wilderness years and his previous failures helped sustain him. He wasn't going to give in. In his own way, he became a *senex* for a nation.

Thomas Cole's series of four paintings, entitled *The Voyage of Life*, describe the four phases of life. For me, the third painting is the most stunning, the picture of a man in the middle of life in a boat with a storm going on, the tiller missing, feeling out of control.

The final picture is a portrait of old age. The waters are calm, the boat is battered, the figure is withered. The lush landscape of youth is gone—only some rocks remain. But the man is joyous again, knowing that faith has sustained him, and he is heading toward the borders of death to a new adventure. Much in his life was not as he expected, he had given up much. But in the picture, he has not really given in.

TAKEAWAY:

1. You can let go of a dream without giving in.

2. Diminishment in your life brings paradoxical expansions.

3. We have a different wilderness in the morning of our life than in the afternoon of our life.

4. Perhaps your wilderness will help you become a *senex*.

6

FAILING OVER SUCCEEDING

In God's economy, nothing is wasted. Through failure, we learn a lesson in humility, which is probably needed, painful though it is.

—*As Bill Sees It*, Alcoholics Anonymous

Look where all your work has gotten you. At first they just hated you. Then they called you a traitor. Then they had you beaten. Then they threw you in a dungeon. You were starving, weren't you? When you finally met the king, you had to beg, not much of a prophet after all, and you were moved to the palace prison with a little bit of food. You couldn't sink any lower, could you? Oh, yes you could. Before you knew what was happening, your enemies pulled you out of prison and dropped you into a pit that was about twenty feet deep. It was supposed to hold water, but all it had at the bottom was mud. What a great image

of success you are, sitting there in the dark, sink-
ing deeper and deeper into the mud. How do you
feel now, Jeremiah?

SITTING IN MUD

It is not only failure; it is the fear of failure. Deep within, we want to be recognized as successful, somehow, in some way. It is that impending lack of success that is the killer. We've talked about some of the things that can accompany the wilderness—shame, insignificance, humiliation, bewilderment, and loss. All of these experiences point to failure.

Jeremiah wasn't in a desert, but he was in a kind of wilderness. What does the world look like from the bottom of a dark, muddy, fifteen- to twenty-foot deep pit? Wouldn't it just be easier to say the right things and be honored like the other prophets? What was the use of all this strong talk when the people and the king did not respond? Jeremiah must have felt like such a loser (see Jeremiah 38:1–13).

What is it in us that makes us want so badly to look like we are succeeding? We try to hold up the pretense of worldly success, even in ministry, until we can no longer pretend, covered in mud, at the bottom of a pit. Obvious failure.

Part of my life has been spent listening to people as they spin their pipe dreams. They are in the darkest of pits, yet they are explaining to me how a film contract is just around the corner or how a court settlement will come any day or how they are not really addicted to cocaine, despite how things look right now. It is hard to be honest when facing our own failure. We all find ways to try to avoid the facts.

On the other hand, I have also seen people who would not be judged successes by the world, and yet they have a quiet confidence about them, steadily going about their business.

Why do we fear failure so much? The fear of failure must cut to the core of how we think of ourselves and how we want others to think of us. Yet the experience of failure comes to all of us, one way or another. In fact, in the end, we might see the person who has never known failure as a person to be pitied.

In failure, many of our nightmares come true. We really are as stupid, boorish, and incompetent as we feared. The cousin of failure is self-loathing. Self-loathing is the voice that comes in the midst of failure and says, "See, you've done it again. You really are as pathetic as you expected. Now everyone will know."

Whether we become totally lost in an uncharted region of life—a financial crisis, failed relationship, health tragedy, or moment of huge embarrassment—or are literally sinking in the mud in the dark like Jeremiah, we are in the wilderness. Failure whispers ugly and dark things to us.

We don't like it. No, not at all. In classical New Testament scholarship, we often say the first eight chapters of the Gospel of Mark show Jesus generally as a miracle worker. People are healed. Miracles happen. In the second eight chapters of the book, Jesus is shown generally as a suffering servant. Jesus is betrayed, humiliated, beaten, and killed. It looks like failure—the opposite of miracles. And Jesus doesn't seem to be able to save Himself. In Mark, neither the miracles nor the tragedy are denied. The two experiences are simply both put side by side, the wonder and the ugliness of life. Both aspects are true. It's a paradox.

The end of Mark 8 is a turning point. Jesus tells the disciples that the Son of Man "must suffer many things and be rejected by the elders and the chief priests and the scribes and be killed" (v. 31), all before the Resurrection. What is Peter's reaction? He can't handle that idea of collapse. He took Jesus aside "and began to rebuke him" (v. 32). What Jesus talked about sounded like stunning failure. We don't like the sound of it at all.

GETTING SMALL

In addition to self-loathing, another cousin of failure is the sense of belittlement. The ancient world understood this sense well. Even Aristotle talks about it quite a bit. When we feel as though we have succeeded in something, the comments of others or even mocking have little effect upon us. But when we are uncertain of our success or suspect we have failed, disregard and casual contempt from others can sting and cut. It is one of the primary reasons we might strike out at others. Belittlement can put us on the offense.

When we think we have failed, we sometimes become acutely aware of belittlement from others. We can go to the wilderness facing failure and knowing the world thinks little of us. The word *belittled* itself literally means we become small—be-little-d.

The Bible is full of people who have to face failure and seeming defeat. Hagar wants to raise her child in safety but finds herself instead pushed to a barren land and the very real possibility of death. Moses fails as a prince of Egypt and goes to the desert. The people of God fail to take the Promised Land and so they wander in the desert. David fails to please his king and is driven to the wilderness. Jeremiah should have had the respect due to a prophet, but he's instead dumped unceremoniously into a mud hole. Paul is called to preach the good news to the Gentiles but finds himself in jail. John has so much to say to the churches in Revelation but finds himself imprisoned on an island.

It's a cliché to say that failure can cause a radical examination of our lives. One has to be careful how to say it. Recently I was involved in helping a family dear to me move from Brooklyn. As I pulled a dolly of boxes filled with tiny items, one wheel of the dolly hit a rut and all of the boxes toppled over, and all the little items fell into the dirt. It took a long time, but I picked everything up—threads and needles and buttons and trinkets. I finally started pulling the dolly again and the wheel hit the rut again. Everything toppled out a second time.

After picking everything up piece-by-piece a second time, my grown son passed me with a pile of boxes. I thought, *Here is a chance to show my vulnerability*. I said, with just a touch of false humility, "I've knocked these boxes completely over twice on the same trip out here, but, you know, son, I have learned that my failures are my teachers."

My son, without missing a beat, simply said, "Dad, if that is true, you must be the smartest man in the world." Maybe I am.

Failure does often cause us to reexamine our lives. It can be our teacher. If our life has been going on a certain trail and an incident makes the whole cart turn over and spill onto the road, it might make us think in a different way. In one sense, the Bible is a book of spectacular defeats. Now we look back at the failures in the Bible and value them. But on the whole, in our own lives, we really don't ever want to have even the opportunity to value our failure.

IS FAILURE CONTAGIOUS?

For more than thirty years, on Wednesday nights, our mission has hosted a meal, and anyone is welcome to come. People who have done really well in life are with us—also people who are homeless, who have mental health issues, who have had drug and alcohol problems, who have physical disabilities. If someone from another part of the country comes to help us, sometimes I can see our Wednesday group from their perspective. Sometimes the people bring pity and feel as though they have walked into a room full of failures.

I don't see it that way. Because they are my family, I see the wisdom that comes from devastating defeat. I see the courage that comes from sometimes overwhelming cruelty. I see the humor that comes from being the friend of failure. I see the distinctive perspectives that come from being outside the conventional expectations.

To be in the wilderness is to become the friend of failure. It is no longer something to be avoided. When we are adolescents, we don't really want to be around people who are social failures. Perhaps it is contagious. But as we grow older, we see that people who don't know failure don't know how to handle life. People who only know success can be two-dimensional.

Failure, by long or short roads, usually leads us back to the land of grace. In the desert night, we can ask again, "Am I only valued if I am successful? Is there a love that transcends my petty record of ups and downs in my handful of decades in life?"

Sometimes in our group time on Wednesday night, we will say, "I may fail, but I am not a failure." Do I have value even though my life has mostly been a defeat and a betrayal? A certain strength can arise from this up-close experience of failure. Failure can lead to a certain light-hearted humility that cringes at no humiliation.

Jacob of the Bible leads a checkered path through youth and through the wilderness. His early life doesn't bode well for much of a sense of integrity. He takes advantage of his brother and gains his brother's privileges for being the firstborn. Then he connives with his mom to deceive his blind dad and pretends he is his brother in order to get the special blessing, which should have been for the older son. His brother is furious and plans to kill him.

Jacob has to run away. He has deserts to cross. He is on his own. He no longer has his mother to support him, any flocks or resources, or any stable environment. As he camps out, he doesn't have anything but a stone for a pillow. He is running away because he truly is what his name

Jacob indicates—a cheater, cheating those who are closest to him. In the moral sense, he has failed.

And yet as he camps out, soaked in moral failure, he receives a glorious epiphany—a stairway from heaven. God's presence is there, and God speaks words of abundance, blessing, and hope. How can that be? Well, in one sense, in the midst of his failure, Jacob learns that some of the best gifts in life cannot be earned, only given. It is a moment of grace.

Does Jacob get it? Not really—he offers a little bargain with God, if God does these certain things, then Jacob will . . . tithe. Jacob has a way to go, but he is on the road, and the road led through the wilderness of one kind of failure (Genesis 28:10–22).

We all sense that failure can lead to a certain strength, though we keep working to avoid that path to strength. Failure can make us realize new things in prayer. Ignatius, a leader in prayer in the sixteenth century, emphasized cultivating a sense of detachment in prayer, a sense of yielding all our personal hopes of outcomes up to God as we pray. In many ways, a certain power comes when our prayers are not bound to our personal needs or what we think God should do. In a sense, failure in business, ministry, or family can pry loose all our limited plans for what should be happening in the world. Failing can open and empty us of all the things we think God should be doing. It then allows us to be filled with what God might do.

LIFE'S MORE LIKE A TREE THAN A LADDER

I want my life to be like a ladder—rung by rung, neat little squares, heading in one direction, a direction I understand to be "up." However, life is more like a tree—organic, with twists and turns, some expected and some not, complex, and with branches turning in directions I never expected.

Yes, it is moving upward, but not in the neat little squares I planned. And if I treat it like a ladder, something dead and inanimate, breaking off its branches, forcing it to my purposes, I can kill it. Failure reminds me of that.

Even in business, the stated goals are not the way many corporations became successful. DuPont, one of the world's largest chemical companies and the developer of Teflon, Kevlar, and Corian, started out as a gunpowder mill. Tiffany & Co., now best known for its jewelry, started as a "fancy goods emporium" centered on stationery. Coca-Cola, originally developed as a patent medicine, became a nonalcoholic soft drink during Prohibition.

Go figure. Even business, with its proclaimed emphasis on achieving corporate goals, does not move ahead in a straight line like a ladder. There are twists and turns one would never expect.

Going through the wilderness, facing our own failure and personal defeats, reminds us of the unexpected way life develops. In fact, failure often serves as the spectacles to help us see the world.

A third cousin to failure is loneliness. Jacob leaves his family and travels hundreds of miles alone. On Hagar's second trip to the desert, she is ejected from the community. Being alone, trying to protect her child, looks to her like death unless she can find help. Moses runs away from Egypt and all the personal support of being part of the royal community. He also loses his Hebrew community and family. David runs away from certain death and finds himself without a friend in the hostile Philistine community.

Even if one's personal wilderness doesn't involve solitude, we often feel no one understands the magnitude of our feelings of defeat. Failure, in its own way, tries to make you feel all alone. As the old adage goes, "It's not a problem until it is your problem." Others can often be sympathetic, but they are not there in the dark with you at 2:00 in the morning. In the end, the sympathizers are not the ones who failed.

We all know the feeling when friends come to comfort but end up accusing instead. Job's friends started out comforting. Eventually they instructed Job on the reasons for his failure. It all seemed so clear to them. Job couldn't help but feel even more alone.

Self-loathing, belittlement, loneliness—facing our own failure and personal negligence and even crushing disappointment in life is like facing a death. But it would be unrealistic if we did not speak of what can happen on the other side. "Unless a grain of wheat falls into the earth and dies, it remains alone; but if it dies, it bears much fruit," Jesus says (John 12:24). Jesus, the master of paradox, keeps speaking in His upside-down way: "Whoever loves his life loses it" (v. 25).

Jesus' own story is the story branded on our lives—dereliction, abandonment, betrayal, complete failure on the Cross. Both fully divine and fully human, we see a real man asking why God has abandoned Him. Yet there is something on the other side of the failure. In fact, as we look at the Cross, that utter puzzle, that rack of riddles, we see that somehow Jesus had to fail in order to succeed, to be crushed in order to see us thrive.

BABYSITTING IN A GRAVEYARD

At one point in our mission's work in New York City, it seemed as though everything was going wrong. People who had accepted Christ were falling away. The drug trade in the abandoned buildings seemed to thrive. Members of our mission shouted at me on the street, angry because I hadn't done what they expected. I felt as though I was a complete failure, worse than a failure—a joke.

At this time, I was traveling with my wife, and for a while, I was in charge of taking care of our two young children while my wife did some errands in a small town in the Northeast. In the middle of the town was a graveyard. I walked around the graveyard, one young child on my back, the other holding my hand. The tombstones were really old. The faded names went back hundreds of years.

I walked around the graveyard with my children and looked at the names. Were these people successful? Certainly there were no names I knew—no George Washingtons or Thomas Jeffersons or Dolly Madisons. They were nothings, just names on faded stone. Even the print on the stones had begun to fade, making them hard to read. I began to ask myself again, "What does it mean to be a success, anyway?" Maybe my mind would not have gone there if I were not swimming in my own incompetence in ministry. It was a brooding moment.

Strangely enough, a lightheartedness came over me. I began to think of all the worries and anxieties that each of these people in the graveyard once had. I wondered at their own sense of failure in the dark times, whether they ever felt as depressed as I did. I realized no one knew those worries or self-incriminations now. They were all forgotten by the world. They didn't really matter as much as the people thought they did. As I looked at the tombstones, I realized my little concerns didn't matter that much either. Someday no one will remember.

Funny how life has these twists and turns. Spending time in the cemetery cheered me up far more than if I had gone to an amusement park.

Another cousin of failure is despair. But despair can lead to a new beginning. On reflection, despair can be very self-centered. Despair sees the world through the lens of its own accomplishments, and the world is much bigger than that. As we mentioned before, in the end, despair presumes to know that nothing good can ever come out of the current wilderness situation. On further thinking, a hidden arrogance resides in that kind of despair. How can anyone ever be so presumptuous as to make such a statement? Remember, life is more like a tree anyway. It doesn't have the even rungs of a ladder, moving steadily toward a goal. Twists and turns are part of the deal. And we don't get to change the deal. As one old saying goes, "God doesn't say, 'Let's make a deal.' He says 'This is the deal.'"

Jeremiah must have felt like total failure. Reviled by his community, imprisoned, dropped into a pit, sinking in the mud, starving—nothing looked successful at the time. Jeremiah may have had a propensity toward the darker view anyway. At one point, he cursed the day he was born and wished he had died in the womb (Jeremiah 20:17). Wow. Yet as we look at his life now, he was not a failure.

Alcoholics Anonymous has a lot of experience with failure and with success. I have heard members of AA use this statement, "How you are feeling is not necessarily a good indication of how you are doing." In the original context, of course, a person can be drinking and feeling great, yet he has abandoned his wife, children, and job and is not doing well at all. In another sense, like Jeremiah, we may be feeling like a failure, but we may be in the finest hour of our life in terms of how we are doing. Time in a personal wilderness sometimes helps us see that other side of things.

In that upside-down way, one sometimes moves to a different side of failure. We so often live our lives in the imagination of others, striving to justify or impress those around us. Failure helps us reconsider our motivations. Is our motive really to please this person or that group? In our Bible studies at the mission, sometimes we will ask the question, "Who holds your report card in their pocket?" A parent, a lover, a clique, a concept?

Some of the most confident people I have ever met on the streets of New York City have experienced the most failure. Funny how that works. I am thinking about one person who had known homelessness, prisons, and mental institutions—he had failed in many of the ways society deemed failure. So why did he have this quiet confidence about him? He had turned his life over to Christ, and he saw from experience that failure did not determine who he was. A temporary failure did not distract him. He had known worse. He did not fear failure because failure had taught him he had a value beyond failure.

AN EMPTY ROOM AND A NEW START

Catherine Doherty was a woman of prayer and compassion. She did not have an easy life. She married at fifteen and was forced to leave Russia after the Russian Revolution. She found herself nearly starving to death in Finland before she and her husband made it to Canada. She always seemed to have a heart for God, and because of her travels, she was steeped in both Eastern and Western Christian traditions. She was articulate and soon entered the lecturing circuit in the United States. Things seemed to stabilize in her life.

Then her world began to fall apart. Battling poverty, she separated from her husband. She was able to gain recognition as a speaker in the intervening years, and though she grew out of poverty, she was not at peace. She could not overcome the conviction that Christ had called her to sell her possessions and follow Him. And she did just that, choosing to live in the slums of Toronto.

She would talk about setting up a special room or place that was spare, with no distractions—perhaps a table, a chair, a bed, a Bible, and a cross, but that was it. This would be a place for people to step away from their normal patterns and distractions and experience Christ in silence and emptiness and in His fullness.

One of the books in which she wrote about these little bare rooms became a classic on prayer. She took a word from the Russian Christian tradition. She used that word as the title of the book. The word originally indicated a geographical place, but eventually it described the spare room set aside for a person to simply pray with no distractions. That word became the description of this whole approach to prayer and has helped a new generation of people who have also experienced breakdown and who consequently hunger for something more.

That word hints at the defeat and emptiness and prayer and rebirth she experienced. The word was *poustinia*. Sure enough, in Russian, the word means "wilderness" or "desert."

TAKEAWAY:

1. The four cousins of failure are self-loathing, belittlement, loneliness, and despair.

2. Failure can become a teacher when it causes us to reexamine things.

3. We see that life has twists and turns, more like a tree than a ladder.

4. Ironically, facing failure in the wilderness can lead to a fruitful confidence.

7

Developing Wait Training

Time is also a servant of the Lord.

—attributed to Watchman Nee

So how long is this going to go on? You made a promise to me that things would go well. When I followed your instructions, the first thing I encountered was lack and famine for me and my relatives. You promised I would have many children, but my wife has none. It just seems to go on and on, month after month, year after year, and nothing changes. I am getting older. And so is she. So what am I supposed to do, anyway? I have been faithful, haven't I? Well, mostly. It's bad enough that I have the name, Abram, "exalted father," when my poor wife has no children. This always makes things awkward when I am introducing myself. What's worse, now You've given me a new name, Abraham, short for "father of a multitude." Right. Sarah still has no children, and she is really old. I mean really old. We have been waiting so many years for Your promise. Are You making fun of me with that name? I don't get it. How long will this go on, Lord?

How Long Can This Last?

The elevator smelled like urine. Surely you could find somewhere else to go to the bathroom. My wife, my coworker, and I were visiting someone in the housing projects years ago, and we were joking around as we went to an upper floor. My coworker jumped up and down in the elevator. She was about five-foot-two and weighed ninety pounds. I am six-foot-four and weigh two-hundred pounds. I decided I could jump up and down in the elevator too. The moment my massive bulk hit the floor of the elevator, it stopped. Right in the middle of the floors. We waited. We shouted for help. Nothing. Again and again. Nothing. We had no cell phones. There was no emergency phone in the enclosure.

Surely someone would help us. Silence. We sang songs. We told jokes. As time dragged on, I needed to go to the bathroom too. I began to understand why the elevator smelled as it did. The three of us wouldn't say it, but we began to think we might just be left there forever. Decades later they might check on that old, nonfunctioning elevator that had been out of use for so long, and they might find our spindly skeletons in there, jaws open, shouting for help to the end. Despair began to seep into the corners of our little enclosure. Time dragged on. We called out, but no one was there.

Finally, we heard a thin voice from above shout, "Don't worry! We'll get you out!" That was all. It took them some time, but after that, everything changed. We were still waiting, but it was a different kind of waiting. I learned that there are two kinds of waiting—waiting when you don't know when things will end and waiting when you see an end in sight.

A lot of our life feels like that first kind of waiting. Perhaps we started with the assurance of a promise, but time drags on, and the promise seems to recede and eventually evaporate. All we have left are the four walls around us and perhaps the hint of a smell of a restroom.

Perhaps we will be like Abraham. We receive a promise that we will be a great nation, but the months and the years drag on. No time schedule seems to have been given. Age creeps in, the body wastes, and we aren't sure of the next phase. We only know nothing has happened yet. Finally, finally, when the special child came for Abraham, we realize he never saw his offspring become as numerous as the sand on the shore or the stars in the heavens. That all happened after he died. He didn't see it.

The Bible is full of that kind of waiting followed by incomplete fulfillment in this life. The promise is completed, but we don't see it, or we don't see all of it. Moses got to the Promised Land, but he didn't enter it in this life. Paul planned to go to Spain, but we are not sure he got there.

One of the primal cries of the human heart is "How long?" How long will this suffering continue? How long will I have this financial challenge? How long will I have to endure this excruciating pain? How long will those against me do so well, and how long will I do so poorly? How long will this depression last? How long will I be lonely? How long will the promises of God seem empty rather than be fulfilled? How long will my life look like a joke? How long will I struggle with the same weakness, over and over, year after year?

It helps when the doctor says, "This will only hurt for a moment." But what if the doctor can't say that? What if we don't know when the pain will stop or, worse yet, if the pain will stop? Ever?

"How long?" is also one of the most primal heart cries in the Bible. In the Psalms, in Habakkuk, in Job, in Revelation, the people cry, in one way or other, "How long?"

"I'M GOING TO THE GYM"

Time may be one of the hardest things to get our mind around. The brilliant teacher and philosopher Augustine put it this way more than 1,500 years ago: "What then is time? If no one asks me, I know what it is. If I wish to explain it to him who asks, I do not know." Time heals, time surprises, time tests, time makes one forget, time makes one frustrated.

A family member of mine was diagnosed with an aggressive form of cancer. He slowed down and enjoyed every day. He had always been fascinated by physics. He would pose this question to me—What is time, anyway? Albert Einstein himself once wrote in a letter to a friend that past and future were illusory. When death seems closer, sometimes time also seems to slow down.

Time helps us become aware. We become aware of what is important to us. We become aware of our limitations. We are able to evaluate. God can use time, as God can use so many things, to form and shape our character.

Some things just don't change except through time. A friend at our mission used to say, "God uses a slow cooker more than He does a microwave."

We know there is a training component to time. Of course, I want all difficulties to disappear immediately, but the Bible tells us that testing produces steadfastness (James 1:3) and suffering produces endurance and endurance produces character (Romans 5:3–4). Our inner world changes as time progresses. We don't exactly understand how.

One of my coworkers in New York City spent part of his life in mental institutions, part of his life in crack houses, and part of his life living in the park. Christ transformed him, and the wisdom from his difficult times gave him a great peace. When testing and delays happened in my coworker's life, he would say, "I am going to the gym." I get it. Time, like a heavy weight, strengthens the muscles of the soul. Time helps, so to speak, in "wait training."

Some cultures honor this attentive waiting more than our culture does. For a while, I had a Japanese painting of a shrike poised on a reed, totally still, balanced, waiting for its prey. The shrike's waiting was not inactivity—it was a quiet and firm anticipation of what was going to happen next. This kind of waiting is something our society has at times devalued. We don't know how to do it.

The wilderness in the Bible is often a time of waiting. The normal activities and equipment of life have been withdrawn. We are not seeing anything happening. At first, perhaps this lack of normal activity is frustrating, but as we wait, as we are quiet, a sense of presence can come, a sense of quiet purpose. Our perspective is reoriented.

Could Paul talk about contentment if he had not spent so many days and months forced into inactivity in jails around the Mediterranean? Would Abraham have been as strong a leader if he had seen an immediate answer to the promises God made to him? Who would Abraham have been if he had not seen famine right after the promise of blessing, if he had not waited year after year for the promise of a child through Sarah, if he had not made mistake after mistake, lying about his wife to the authorities and having a child by another woman trying to make the promise happen? Worst of all, in the end, he was told to assume a name (father of nations) that seemed to promise so much and yet extravagantly flaunted his failure.

The Bible doesn't explain what went on in Abraham's mind. We can't help but remember the later test to Abraham, when he finally has Isaac and is told to sacrifice him. In this troubling story, the command of God seems to conflict with the gracious promise of God. Could Abraham have said, "God will provide," with such purpose without the years of waiting he had already experienced? The Bible doesn't say.

THE EMPTY PROMISES OF GOD

Recently a friend who is a minister in New York City had a wretched summer. One of the people he had poured his life into was rejecting God. He had to put his faithful dog to sleep. A worker that had shown so much promise was unfairly kicked out of the house. He was spending up to twelve hours a day in a hospital room waiting for some signs of recovery of a friend who had been shot in the head and was now in a coma. He was exhausted. He used a phrase that perhaps many in the Bible could agree with. He said he was experiencing the "empty promises of God."

Abraham could have felt that way sometimes, with the powerful promise given to him and years in which there was no empirical evidence the promises would be fulfilled. Joseph could have understood, with the powerful dreams he had and the following slavery and imprisonment. David could have understood, with the anointing as king and then years of running like a fugitive. Even Jesus, in a way, could understand, coming as the Messiah and then being condemned and mocked by the people of God. Perhaps the phase of experiencing that empty promise is a part of the journey to the remarkable fulfillment of so many things. There is a time between the promise and the fulfillment that involves either waiting or quitting.

The wilderness will have an effect on us when we're in the in-between times. Either the circumstances change or we change. Sometimes the circumstances don't change until we change. Sometimes we don't ever see any prospect of change in the circumstances, but we still change. Sometimes if we knew exactly when the wilderness would end, it wouldn't really be the wilderness.

I have realized that some things don't ever change in this life. We talk about the abundance of Christ, and yet the disciples' lives did not end peacefully. I have sat with a prisoner in jail, and I don't see much hope for that person. Mental illness, destructive patterns, depression, shattered health—all make the prospects so bleak. Even then, however, I can tell them about a time when God will wipe every tear from their eyes, and there will be no more crying or pain. Just not yet.

Waiting touches a core resistance in our inner life. We want to be in charge. We always have. In the earliest story, we want to take control, to be "like God" (Genesis 3:5); as if control is something we can take away from God.

Thomas à Kempis, a fifteenth-century priest, advised to pray this prayer to God: "Give what You will, as much as You will, and when You will." To pray "give what you will" is hard. To pray "as much as you will" can sometimes be even harder. But to pray "when you will" is perhaps the hardest. In the in-between time, in the wilderness, to wait and to wait and to wait touches our urge for controlling time. We feel we can't do it. Sometimes peace is only on the other side of submission to "wait training."

A fascinating rhythm of living occurs in the lives of people of faith in the Bible. We see it over and over again. Here's what happens—the promises that sometimes seemed least answered are most granted.

Abraham and Sarah get the promise that they will be a great nation, and they encounter famine, conflict, and, year after year after year, barrenness. Jacob is the grandson of Abraham, and he finds himself on the run with no support, having nothing out in the wild and using a stone as a pillow. Joseph has amazing dreams of superiority over his family and finds himself a slave and eventually a prisoner. David gets anointed as the future king and then finds himself a fugitive for years. Jesus gets the affirmation from God who is pleased with Him as His beloved Son, and yet the very people of God resist Him, try to trick Him, eventually arrest Him, mock Him, beat Him, and kill Him. The promises for each of these people seem least answered yet Abraham, Sarah, and Jacob have offspring that eventually come to a point where billions look to them as a beginnings of their faith. Joseph's amazing act as prime minister of Egypt eventually saves the known world from hunger and keeps Judah alive (the line of David and the line of Jesus). David is remembered as the great king in the line of Jesus. Jesus . . . well, the story of Jesus is not over.

Some answers to prayers, some fulfillment of promises, we will never see. Abraham never saw his offspring like the stars of the sky or the sand of the sea. That all happened after his death. Jesus told the disciples that He brought life abundantly, and yet nearly all of them were killed or imprisoned. Many things in our lives will seem like a riddle until they are put in the context of eternity. The here and the now will not make sense sometimes unless there is a beyond. One's point of view always depends on one's point of viewing. Recognizing the beyond is not the "opiate of the people" as some indicate. In fact, sometimes denying the beyond can become an opiate.

SCRAPS OF PAPER WITH SCRIPTURE

Sometimes we see a hint of the fulfillment of things we have waited for and endured for a long time. Stories are what keep us going through the waiting time. One of the stories we have told to each other at our mission church comes from Russia, as told by Nik Ripken and Barry Stricker in The Insanity of Obedience. This has helped us through some "wait training" times.

This is the true story of Dmitri, who lives in a small village about a four-hour drive from Moscow. Dmitri was born and raised in a believing family and went to church as a child. But slowly communism eliminated most of the churches of worship in his area. Some of the pastors were imprisoned and killed.

By the time he was an adult, the nearest church building was a three-day walk away, and Dmitri and his family were only able to go once or twice a year. Dmitri and his wife decided that, even though they had no religious training, they would gather their sons once a week and read the Bible together and give them a little training, since the boys had so little church experience.

Dmitri read the stories in the Bible, and then he would try to explain what he read. Soon the whole family would help each other tell and retell the stories. Before long, the boys asked if they could sing together some of the traditional songs they had heard in the church in the rare times they could visit. It was natural that they began to pray as they sang and read the Bible together and explained the stories.

They lived in a small village. The houses were close together and the neighbors heard them when they sang. A few people asked if they could come listen to the Bible stories and sing the old songs together. By the time about twenty-five people began to gather, the authorities took notice. They told Dmitri, "You have started an illegal church!"

Dmitri responded, "I have no religious training. This is not a church building. We simply get together, sing the songs, tell some stories, and perhaps gather some money to give to a poor neighbor when we can. How can you call that a church?"

The authorities would physically threaten Dmitri. They said, "It looks like a church to us. If you don't stop it, bad things are going to happen."

When the group grew to fifty people, Dmitri was fired from his factory job. His wife lost her teaching position. His boys were expelled from school.

When the group grew to seventy-five people, there was not enough room for everyone to sit. The villagers stood shoulder-to-shoulder, and some stood outside, listening through the windows to the singing and the man of God sharing from the Bible.

One night as they gathered, the door burst open, and an official and soldiers pushed their way into the house. The official slapped Dmitri across the face, over and over, and slammed him against the wall in front of the gathered villagers. He said, "We will not warn you again. If you do not stop this nonsense, this is the least that is going to happen to you."

As the official pushed his way toward the door, one brave grandmother took her life in her hands and stepped in front of him. Like an Old Testament prophet, she looked the official in the eye, and said, "You have placed your hands on a man of God, and you will not survive."

This all happened on a Tuesday night. On Thursday night, the officer had a heart attack and dropped dead. At the next house church meeting, more than 150 people showed up. The authorities couldn't let this continue, and Dmitri went to jail.

Then came the waiting. And more waiting. His family endured great poverty and hardship. The authorities moved Dmitri hundreds of miles away and locked him in a tiny cell where he could hardly take a step. The worst part of the experience was not the foul open toilet in one corner of the cell, or the cracked sink, but that, according to Dmitri, he was the only believer among 1,500 hardened criminals.

The physical torture was brutal, but what kept Dmitri from breaking were two disciplines he learned from his father. Every morning for seventeen years while he was in the prison, he would face east and raise his arms to praise God, and then he would sing his song, a special "heart song," to Jesus.

You can imagine how the other prisoners reacted. They laughed, they cursed, they jeered. They banged their cups against the bars and shouted for him to shut up. They threw food or even human waste to make him be quiet. They did everything they could to keep him from singing his special song in that dark place at dawn.

Dmitri's second discipline was a habit. Whenever he found a small scrap of paper, no matter how small, he would sneak it back to his cell. He would take a stub of a pencil or a piece of charcoal and scrawl a Scripture verse or a Bible story on it. He wrote as small as he could so he could fit as much as he could on the scrap. Then Dmitri would place it on a concrete pillar in his cell that leaked constantly. While his cell was always wet or covered with ice, Dmitri would stick the scrap of paper on the pillar, as high as he could, as an offering of praise to God.

When the jailors spotted the scrap of paper, they would come into the cell, beat Dmitri, and take it down. But no matter what the guards or the other prisoners did, Dmitri continued to practice these two disciplines.

The years continued in the prison. While he waited, his family suffered terribly. The jailers led him to believe at one point that his wife had been murdered and his children taken by the state. They told him they had ruined his home.

It was not only the waiting. It was the uncertainty. What had happened to his family? Finally Dmitri's resolve broke. He told God he couldn't take it anymore. He told the jailers that they had won. "You win," he said. "I must get out and find out what happened to my children." He didn't know what to do. Nothing made sense.

The jailers told him that they would prepare the confession that night, and he could sign it in the morning. Then he could go free. All Dmitri had to do was to sign his name on a document that said he was not a believer in Jesus Christ but was a paid agent of the Western governments who were trying to destroy the USSR. Once he signed, he was free to go.

The waiting, the uncertainty, and the wilderness had defeated Dmitri. He said, "Bring it tomorrow, and I will sign it." That night was a night of deep despair. Dmitri had given up.

Hundreds of miles away, Dmitri's wife, children, and Dmitri's brother sensed through the Holy Spirit Dmitri's anguish and uncertainty. That night, they got in a circle and prayed out loud for Dmitri. Miraculously, the Holy Spirit allowed Dmitri to hear the voices of his loved ones there in his jail cell.

The next morning, the guards brought in the documents for Dmitri to sign. Dmitri's back was straight, and he looked them in the eye. "I'm not signing anything," he said.

The guards couldn't believe it. "What happened?" they demanded.

"Last night God let me hear the voices of my wife and my children. They are together. You lied to me. I now know my wife is alive and well and my sons are with her and that they are still in Christ. I am signing nothing."

The guards continued to work to discourage him. One day in the prison, Dmitri was overwhelmed by a special gift from God. He found a whole piece of paper, not a scrap. To his great joy, a whole pencil lay beside it.

In great happiness, Dmitri filled both sides of the paper with Scripture verses. He carefully placed it on the concrete pillar as a very special praise to God. The guards, when they found it, were furious. They beat Dmitri and threatened him with execution.

Dmitri was dragged down the central corridor toward the place of execution when the strangest thing happened.

Before they reached the outer courtyard—1,500 hardened criminals stood at attention by their beds. They faced the east, raised their arms, and made what to Dmitri sounded like an angelic chorus. Fifteen-hundred prisoners sang Dmitri's heart song, the one they had heard him sing every morning for so many years.

The guards stopped, released their hold on Dmitri and stared at him in terror. "Who are you?" they demanded.

Dmitri straightened up, and said with confidence, "I am a son of the Living God, and Jesus is His name!"

The jailers returned him to his cell. Sometime later, he was released from the prison. He returned to his village and to his family.

The story goes on. The part that touched me most was the fact that, once again, the prayers that seemed least answered in the wilderness are sometimes most granted. Things have changed. The prison, where Dmitri was incarcerated for almost two decades, now has a chaplain. The chaplain is Dmitri's own son, who had such a hard time, growing up without his father.

TAKEAWAY:

1. There are two kinds of waiting—waiting when you don't know when it will end and waiting when you do.

2. "How long?" is a primal heart cry in the Bible.

3. Sometimes waiting strengthens the muscles of patience—a kind of weight training for the heart.

4. The fact that the promises of God seem empty in the wilderness may be part of their fulfillment.

5. The prayers that seem least answered in the wilderness are sometimes most granted.

8

REFUSING TO MAKE THINGS HAPPEN

He who has not been brought low, reduced to nothing through the cross and suffering, takes credit for works and wisdom and does not give credit to God. . . . He, however, who has emptied himself through suffering no longer does works but knows that God works and does all things in him.

—Martin Luther

You got all anxious again, didn't you? You thought you could take charge, but in the end, you just resented those who didn't work as hard as you did. Before you knew it, your angry thoughts bubbled out in public. You blamed your sister, and you blamed Jesus. You didn't look like the gracious host after all. Things turned out to be just the opposite of what you expected. Way to go, Martha.

A Woman Engulfed in Books

Martha liked to make things happen. So do I. Some people don't want to sit still. One test conducted by the University of Virginia and Harvard University found many people would rather receive an electric shock than sit still for fifteen minutes. In the end, Martha was so mad at her sister she went in and tried to get a third party to get Mary moving. Martha turned to Jesus. Surely He could get her going. It didn't work (Luke 10:38–42).

When I first arrived in New York City, a woman changed my life through her insights. I am an avid reader. My office and apartment are filled with books. My son says that any place I stay, I "bookify" it. Linda, who lived in the Lower East Side, was also a reader . . . times ten. In fact, she had read more books than just about anyone I had ever met. She was not a professor in some university. In fact, for a number of years, she had lived in an abandoned building a block away from our mission.

She didn't own a lot, except for books. By the time I met her she had an apartment. She helped cook a meal for the homeless at the mission every week. She sat in every Bible study and knitted. She had seen trouble in her life—an abusive husband, a landlord in her abandoned building who had her beaten with a tire iron, a son who was sometimes violent toward her. In her own way, she was brilliant. You couldn't bring up a book she hadn't read. Every corner of her apartment was stuffed with old books and paperbacks. Going to visit her to drink tea was an experience one didn't forget.

It is strange how sometimes one sentence stays with you and changes the way you look at things. I was going through a rough time in my own life. People were angry at me. Every part of my life seemed to be stuck in neutral. I felt as though I was on the slowest track, and everyone else was on the inside track, racing past me.

Linda made this comment as she drank her tea, surrounded by books. She had read just about every Christian author I knew, people who had written from the second century on. She said, "This is what I am learning. I am learning to allow things to happen rather than to make things happen."

In an upside-down way, the wilderness reminds us we are not the captain of our ship, and probably not really the master of our fate, as we had supposed. The wilderness comes in many forms—a sense of purposelessness and wandering, a separation from our friends, a lack of resources. It can be exacerbated by sickness, imprisonment, inactivity, a deep inability in a hard situation. All these things can make us stop and realize we don't really make things happen.

Sometimes we try to make things happen in inappropriate ways. When God's promise doesn't come in the time and way we think it should, when we set a time boundary on God and feel like He has not come through, we take things in our own hands. When Sarah and Abraham saw they were not having a child, Sarah decided to help the situation by presenting her servant Hagar to Abraham. Ishmael was the result, and a lot of problems ensued.

When God's purpose and protection don't seem clear to us in our time schedule, sometimes we attempt to make things happen by working harder. Jesus never said that if you are busy enough, you can move mountains. When things don't work out, instead of stopping, we work harder. Then the wilderness comes in a deeper way. We see our emptiness and inability more clearly. We are not a captain of our ship. We are only a passenger.

THE PRAYER OF RELINQUISHMENT

There are many kinds of prayers. Author Catherine Marshall talks about the prayer of relinquishment. She learned about it while in a sort of wilderness herself. She had a lung infection and the doctors could do nothing about it. She prayed for health, using all the faith she could muster, but after six months, she was still in bed. Day after day.

One day she read a story of a prayer of a missionary who had been an invalid for eight long years. Finally the missionary said something like this—"All right. I give up. If You want me to be an invalid, that is Your business. Anyway, I want You more than I want health. You decide." In two weeks the missionary was out of bed and completely well.

Catherine Marshall decided to pray the same prayer. On a specific day, she came to a point of total acceptance. In a few hours, she sensed the presence of Christ in a new way, and her recovery began, wiping away her doubt.

Catherine saw that a demanding spirit, full of self-will, can block the Spirit. It took six months in bed to get her to a point of seeing the way. She learned more about different kinds of prayer. Jesus' prayer on the night He was betrayed and about to die touches this kind of prayer—"Not my will, but yours" (Luke 22:42).

It is easy to say that the best things are not earned but received. It takes time to feel it in our bones. Occasionally it takes a wilderness.

The Bible teachers of the reformation thought a lot about this. Martin Luther looked at the categories in his own time—he described them as the active life or the contemplative life. He said there was a third choice—the passive life. This third way recognizes that we are not the prime initiator. We want to be. We will use anything to create the illusion that we are the prime mover. We will even use religious things, using "God against God." But in this different understanding, which is the passive life, God is the active subject. Luther emphasized that it was God at work in us by Himself. We do nothing on our own. He specifically pointed out that those who had not experienced suffering—think wilderness—take credit for works and wisdom and do not give credit to God.

In essence, the old self, or as the Bible says it, the old Adam, wants active recognition for itself through what we do. We want to justify ourselves and make ourselves secure through doing (active life) and thinking (contemplative life). In short, we want to be the captains of our own destinies.

Today we may use different categories, but we can understand what Luther is talking about. We are brilliant at finding methods to do things our way. I can even use my supposed humility as a weapon to achieve recognition. We maneuver to get a medal for our humbleness. We talk outwardly about God's will until something in our inner fortress of plans starts to crumble. Then our anger and resentment that things are not as we planned erupts.

In the wilderness experience, the inner fortress of our plans often starts to crumble. It can be devastating, yet something comes from it. A famous motto, sometimes attributed to the general Hannibal as he planned to bring elephants across the Alps to attack the Romans, goes like this—"I will find a way or make one." The motto has been used by many others, and it is an admirable sentiment and very useful in many circumstances. Yet the wilderness experiences of life remind us there are limits to this approach to the world—there are limits to our being the captains of our own destiny.

In our mission church, some use this saying, "Life has a board for every behind." We think we can do it all our way and not be burned, but in reality, we can't. When we think we have achieved it, life, in the form of the wilderness, comes around the corner. By wandering in a real or metaphorical desert, we experience that most fundamental of human realities we often try to deny—"I am not in charge."

We want to foster the dream that we are in charge. The serpent gives Eve the promise of that dream in the first pages of the Bible. If you do this thing, you will be like God. Instead, we find ourselves thrust out of the garden, left with a sense of vulnerability and remorse.

DOES THIS TYPE OF LIFE MAKE YOU A SLUG?

The Bible has a lot of ways to describe a life of allowing things to happen rather than making things happen. One of my favorites is found in John 3. In it Jesus describes to the perplexed and literalistic Nicodemus this life he is outlining. He doesn't really give a category, or something that can be held in your hand. It is hard to describe this life with a system of words. Instead, Jesus gave a provocative metaphor. "The wind blows where it wishes, and you hear its sound, but you do not know where it comes from or where it goes. So it is with everyone who is born of the Spirit" (v. 8). This life of allowing things to happen is like the wind. You can't describe it or diagnose it or determine it. In that sense it is a type of passive life.

This type of life does not mean being inactive. It doesn't mean being passive in that sense of the word. This type of life can lead, however, to a deeper listening. The power of life from God flows through us—we cannot manufacture it. Jesus lead in this at the beginning of His ministry when He read from Scripture: "The Spirit of the Lord is upon me, because he has anointed me to proclaim good news to the poor" (4:16). Paul understood this process of the Spirit of Christ flowing through us when he said, "It is no longer I who live, but Christ who lives in me" (Galatians 2:20).

The end of Peter's life has been a source of meditation on action and the passive life. Peter was certainly active— jumping out of the boat to follow Jesus (Matthew 14:29), claiming he would never forsake Him (Matthew 26:33), pulling a sword out to cut off an attacker's ear (John 18:10), and rebuking Jesus when he thought Jesus had gone too far in describing His own death (Matthew 16:22). Peter was not a slug, though his actions were often on the impetuous side.

One of the last things Jesus said to Peter in the Gospel of John relates to activity. "When you were young, you used to dress yourself and walk wherever you wanted," Jesus said. This is the kind of freedom of activity we are used to. "But when you are old, you will stretch out your hands, and another will dress you and carry you where you do not want to go" (John 21:18). How many people have faced a certain kind of wilderness when they have grown older, even if it did not involve imprisonment? It is the wilderness of inactivity, enforced by health or circumstances. Inactivity, especially for active people, can make one challenge the purpose of life. It tends to turn things upside down.

Tradition tells a bit more of the story of Peter. When he was old and in chains in Rome, he was led to his place of crucifixion. Perhaps he had a lot of time to think about his time with Jesus and the time after the earthly Jesus was gone. His impetuosity seems to have been adjusted and turned around. According to tradition, Peter asked to be crucified upside down.

As we reflect on the Biblical ethos, it becomes clear that the core of living is not acting but listening. Both Jesus and Paul are extremely active, but their action is based on allowing God to work in them. One of the mottoes at our mission is "Don't just do something, stand there." The living promise of God to guide us begins to spring up everywhere in the Bible. "And your ears shall hear a word behind you saying, 'This is the way, walk in it,' when you turn to the right or when you turn to the left" (Isaiah 30:21). How practical. The words make one ask, "Why are we not availing ourselves of this?"

This promise, found so many times in the Bible, is the GPS of the ancient world. It shows the way we should go in the times we feel we are in the wilderness: "I will instruct you and teach you in the way you should go; I will counsel you with my eye upon you" (Psalm 32:8).

When we are shoved into any sort of desert in our life, many of the things that keep us going can be withdrawn, from constant activities to the constant blaring of the TV or podcast. Without any outward stimuli, we can return to that passive posture, a posture of real listening. In many of the references in the Bible, the word for listening also implies obeying. As a teenager, I could often hear my parent's instructions, but I was not really listening. Their words were like the teacher's words in a Charlie Brown cartoon—*wah wah wah*.

This is an important distinction in the Bible. I cannot say, "God, show me Your will, and . . . I will consider it as one of my options." God is God. One of the stupidest things we can do is take God for a fool. The wilderness times give us a chance to train, to cultivate our listening posture.

At the end of the Gospel of John, I have written in the margin of my Bible a quote from missionary and literacy advocate Frank Laubach, "Forty-seven times in the Gospel of John, Jesus said He was under God's orders, and that He never did anything, never said anything, until His Father gave the command."

Brother Lawrence, the hero of washing pots and pans in the seventeenth century, was another one that continues to teach our community about listening. He said we stop the flow of God's grace "by the little value we set upon it." Let's stop devaluing that listening posture.

Listening involves being still. We are told to be still (Psalm 46:10), but we don't want to be still for very long. We are like that child who brings his father his broken toy in frustration. The father calmly takes a look at the toy and deliberately takes it to his work desk. The child becomes impatient, waiting as the father begins to repair the toy. "Oh, forget it," the child says, as he snatches the toy out of his father's hands. Being still can be very hard for us, but in an upside-down way, it can be very productive, if we could only understand.

WHAT TO DO WHEN YOU ARE LOST IN THE WOODS

As a missionary in Hong Kong many years ago, I encountered a phase of depression. It stunned me. I had believed I could always enforce mind over matter. I felt I could always make myself cheer up. But I could not. Telling myself to cheer up was like telling someone who had just broken their legs to simply take a brisk walk around the block. Even though I was in a Christian context, I had to face, in a new way, my inability to make things better. I was certainly praying. I was certainly trying to make things better. I was trying, anyway.

One thing that people sometimes say in the East helped me. "Muddy waters, when still, become clear." Being still didn't change my circumstances. I was still depressed. I still felt as though I was in a pathless place, all alone, even though people who loved me were around me. All I could do was be quiet. For me at that time, it was perhaps the best thing I could do.

Years later, I took a survival course in New Jersey, of all places. The teacher was a professional tracker, and he had been called in to track many people who had become lost. Of course, many times, when a person realizes he or she is lost, the first response is to move faster. Sometimes the person starts running frantically. This is often when injury can happen. Fear takes over in some to such a degree that even when they see the rescuer, or even members of their family, their first response is to run. Of course, when one is lost, the first thing to do is to stop. Let things be clear.

If we are fortunate, the wilderness will help us stop. We probably have something new or at least different to learn. The muddy waters will need to become clear again.

We don't want to read about allowing things to happen sometimes. We think that the approach can be an excuse for the lazy, the uncommitted, the unproductive. Yet there is a time for everything. The story of Mary and Martha in the Book of Luke can certainly help us in this respect. Martha is a doer. Clearly she wants to impress her special guest, Jesus. Her sister Mary (that slug!) is simply sitting at Jesus' feet when there is so much to do. Mary's resentment, understandable to me, boils up and blocks her intended purpose, to please her special guest. She ends up rebuking Jesus, telling Him to tell Mary to get off her duff and help out. Seems like the right thing to do to me.

But Jesus takes another path. He acknowledges Martha's anxiety about doing many things. But he says Mary has chosen the one thing necessary. She is still. She is listening. Another one of those shocking stories. It causes one to think. Of course, Jesus is not condemning action, service for others, or paying attention to the guest by providing tangible help. But there is a rhythm to listening and action. Clearly, listening comes first.

People are always saying the world is getting busier and busier. Perhaps they have said it in every generation. Our goals are productivity, accomplishment, and success. The biblical spaces of wilderness and desert are important, in their time and in ours. It can be the first stage of listening.

God is often telling us to do one of two things. He is either telling us to stand still or to move. Moses wanted justice. He killed a man to make it happen. He had to be in the wilderness for a long time. Then God sends him back. Then things happen. At the crisis moment, when the people of God are caught between a powerful army and a sea, Moses tells the people they have only to be still (Exodus 14:14). Then things change, circumstances are different, the water divides, a way out appears, and the people move. Of course, we remember where the people of God move to. Another wilderness.

Being stuck in a wilderness can teach us the rhythm of life. We think we need to act all the time. We think we have to move faster and faster in order to get things done. But the wilderness reminds us of the two commands of God. One is to act. The other is to be still. We often get the two commands in the wrong order.

The desert experience, some kind of forced inactivity, teaches us for the first time what we really have always known. We sometimes think that in order to get things done, we need to get moving. Martha did that with Jesus and with Mary; she was irritated at anyone who wasn't moving with her. A time of quiet, even seeming purposelessness, shows us the deeper truth. In order to get things done, sometimes we need to cease from doing. In order to start, we need to stop.

TAKEAWAY:

1. A time of perceived purposelessness can teach us to allow things to happen rather than to make things happen.

2. One of the most powerful prayers in the wilderness is the prayer of relinquishment.

3. The core of living is not acting but listening.

4. Fear makes us move faster and faster.

5. Quiet listening doesn't mean constant inactivity—it means hearing the rhythm.

9

FINDING THE LITTLE VISION OVER THE BIG VISION

Never before have I written so long a letter. I'm afraid it is much too long to take your precious time. I can assure you that it would have been much shorter if I had been writing from a comfortable desk, but what else is there to do when he is alone in a narrow jail cell, other than write long letters, think long thoughts, and pray long prayers?

—Martin Luther King Jr., "Letter from Birmingham Jail"

You are missing it. You are looking for the grand and you are missing the wonderful. You are pulling up a faulty ideal of what used to be and you are using it to judge everything that is happening now. You are letting yourself get discouraged over what you think should be happening. You are missing this amazing day of small things. You are despising it. Tell them, Zechariah.

SUBTLE AS A FLYING BRICK

Old men who had seen the first Temple wept when they saw the laying of the foundation of the second (Ezra 3:12). Supposedly, it wasn't as big or as grand. But in that time of a smaller vision, not as big as Solomon's, God spoke to His people in a special way.

"Not by might, nor by power, but by my Spirit" (Zechariah 4:6). The people of God had a lot of complicated plans. They had been through a wilderness of exile and pain. Now they were starting again, but things seemed small, very small. God uses several people to speak to them. One of them is Zechariah: "Whoever has despised the day of small things shall rejoice" (v. 10). Sometimes we are in a day of small things, or a season, or an era, but it is not necessary to despise those small things. And even if we do, there is something beyond, much deeper, much wider. Something we hadn't anticipated—a new and different temple with different proportions for a new and different time.

A man I used to know lived in an abandoned building a block away from the mission in New York City. To visit him, you had to pry open some unsecured plywood on a window and climb through. The place was dank and smelly like a cave. The floor was covered with a fine layer of wet dust. This man had once been outwardly successful. He had a family, a job, a house, a life. But he drank to cover a bundle of problems. Slowly the things that supported him were taken away—job, family, house. In the end, he found himself in a park in Manhattan, a place where drugs were easily available, and no one looked down on him because he drank or because he had nothing but the clothes on his back and smelly socks and dirty shoes.

He started coming to a Bible study we had at the mission storefront. He just sat and listened at first. Because of all he had lost, he could see things that had been blocked out earlier in his life. He began to see things differently. His perspective was certainly different from before. His life started to turn around.

"God is as subtle as a flying brick," he would say. "I lost my wife, my kids, my job. God finally got my attention. Now I am listening." That man didn't stay in the abandoned building forever. Eventually his life took a turn for good, and he began to rebuild. But strangely enough, he also brought good for many people who listened to him in a rough neighborhood. He didn't feel sorry for himself. His life had simply gotten more and more limited, and it changed him. He stopped being so self-absorbed. He wanted to help others, to help them learn from what he went through. I have heard those in Alcoholics Anonymous say, "You don't have to wait till the basement to get off the down elevator." This man's experience helped him help others in a way he never would have if he hadn't lost everything. He could tell people, "You don't have to become like me." Life is funny that way. He lost everything and gained a bigger vision in the process. Increasing limitation brought an expansion of vision.

I have pondered on this puzzle of life for more than thirty years. Our mission's Wednesday night meal is open to anyone, as long as no one acts violently toward others. People of all sorts drift in and out. One of our current mottoes is this—don't give food to people; eat with them. Some of the people are homeless for a variety of reasons. Some are mentally ill. Some live in shelters or in assisted living. Some are sad, some are even-keeled, and some are exuberantly happy. It's quite a mix on any given Wednesday. You begin to understand a bit more if you sit down and eat with them.

Sometimes I visit churches that have a great deal of material advantages, churches that help us out in our neighborhood. These people have many of the things the people I work with don't have—a good job and status. Sometimes I have the opportunity to have a meal with them as a church. On any given day in that community, some of the people are exuberantly happy, some are even-keeled, and some are very sad, even tortured inside. Strangely, at least to me, the number of advantages or the number of disadvantages doesn't seem to affect the proportion of emotionally high or low attitudes. In terms of the high and low attitudes, it feels about the same.

Jesus talked a lot about the fact that material things don't necessarily change our attitudes. We do not live by bread alone. Life does not consist in the abundance of possessions. Just like my friend who lived in the abandoned building, insight comes when the material things start winding down to zero.

Why Do We Have So Much Cargo?

Jared Diamond, an American scientist who studies other cultures and has written many books, was asked an interesting question by someone in Papua, New Guinea. Why does our Western civilization, and white people specifically, have so much cargo? Why do we have so many material things? In a superficial way, these things can show that we have a certain kind of power.

However, in the wilderness, these things are often taken away. Our cargo in life, the material things we depend on, no longer support us. In the desert, the cell phones, cars, sofas, laptops, and remote controls are occasionally taken away. Paradoxically, as a consequence, we are sometimes able to "see" more. This is the hardship and the gift of the desert.

One can learn these things by having too little or perhaps by having too much. In a study of lottery winners, the findings indicated that the ones who won the lottery actually had less enjoyment of ordinary things than the control groups who had not won. Perhaps the expectations that money can provide the big things made the little things—a cup of coffee or the light through a window—seem less satisfying.

We all know this truth intuitively—that strange expansion that can come from limitation.

Some strains of mission work and of theology find deep significance in the description of Christ in Philippians 2. *Kenosis* comes from the Greek word *kenoó* to describe this approach. It literally means "empty" or "deprive of content." Christ empties Himself, accepting the limitations of a servant (v. 7). Some even call this the "kenotic theology." Ironically, as one reads the passage in Philippians, one realizes that this limitation brings great expansion. In the end, this limitation on Paul as an apostle, and eventually as the victim of execution, brings great expansion, and Jesus receives a name (or character) that is above every name. We feel this in our bones and know that life is often "kenotic."

Jesus helps us understand this insight—the value of limitation. Who is more expansive than Jesus—going to parties with sinners, touching lepers when everyone else shrinks back, protecting the woman caught in adultery, joining the tax collector in a meal, letting a prostitute wash His feet? Yet Jesus gives instruction that people must enter the narrow way (Matthew 7:13–14). It can't mean just following a bunch of petty rules. He has already talked about the Pharisees and their narrowness in piety. He does seem to indicate that by accepting limitations, eventually expansion comes.

We rarely enjoy the deserts in our lives, at least at first. It may be a loss of a loved one, an activity, a job, or a position. Yet in retrospect, we often admit, ironically, that loss brings vision. Winding down engenders a different kind of ramping up.

Personally, some of the most fulfilled people I know are people who limited themselves and their resources to help the poor. How can that be? They have no guarantee that they have enough money to afford rent for the month. A medical expense becomes a burden. They have to watch their pennies if they go to a restaurant. And yet their laughter, their joy in walking with others, is humbling. This fact can seem so obvious, but it seems to be one of the great paradoxes of life, this strange limitation that brings expansion.

Don't Despise the Day of Small Things

When we go into a desert, when we walk in a wilderness, one of the most apparent differences is the lack of the normal amenities we are used to. The comforts, the structures that hold us together in our normal life, are gone. Yet some of us know that a certain peace comes also. We don't have to care about so many things anymore. We don't have so much cargo.

I think travel is more gratifying for some because of this experience—it is at least for me. No car, no garage, no washing machine, no dishwasher, no entertainment center to worry about—just a little suitcase with a toothbrush and a set of clothes to carry. Such a strange joy can come from opening that little suitcase in an unknown place—such a wonderful lack of amenities and clutter.

One time many years ago, I was put in jail as an act of conscience over the forcible removal of the homeless from our park. It was the only time I have been in jail. As I waited in the cell, a quietness came over me. I realized that for once I wasn't in control of anything. I couldn't move, take care of business, call anybody, take care of anyone, or produce anything. All I could do was sit on the bed and maybe talk to my cellmate when he wasn't asleep. There was an odd peace about the whole thing, at least for me, at least for the short time I was there.

Just a room. Earlier in the book, I mentioned the *poustinia* tradition in Russia. In this practice a person starts for a short time in a room, maybe 24 hours. In the room, there is only a bed, a chair, perhaps some bread and water, and a Bible. A *poustinia* room has only three walls, instead of four—one might say. The lack of the fourth wall means one is opened up to an encounter with the divine, the cosmic, the vast—as well as being open to the unexpected guest or experience. As we shared earlier, *poustinia* is the simple Russian word for "desert."

This is one of the secrets of the desert in the Bible too— by limiting things, we experience an expansion. We learn not to flee the "day of small things," as Zechariah says. Rather we seek it. We look to the desert to help us see. Perhaps this understanding is one of the reasons fasting becomes important in our interior journey to see. Jesus went into the desert, and the Bible tells us He did not eat for forty days or forty nights. He purposely limited an activity we understand as essential. In some way, this desert time was a preparation for the movement from being a carpenter to the expanded ministry He was moving toward.

In our mission of doing tangible things for others in the city, we encourage the workers to take time, even a small time, an afternoon or a night, to put other things aside and to just listen. Some have chosen a night out camping with only bread and water. Some have chosen a room on the beach. There are many ways to do this. However, something often happens. By deliberately unplugging, we find ourselves plugged into what is more important. This too is a part of self care. Confirming the vision God has for you helps you know what to do and when.

Part of seeking a place to limit things is hearing again what God says about you. As the truism goes, if you judge a fish by its ability to climb a tree, you will think it is a failure. Stripping things away helps us hear from God who we are and what we are to do. Maybe we are a fish after all and the world is trying to make us act like a squirrel. Finding a desert is one of the ways we see God's invisible love for us again through all the clutter of the carnival of visible circumstances.

ALONE IN THE WOODS AND HATING IT

One of my goals in life now is to encourage those who are doing tangible things for Christ in the city, who are working day in and day out, year by year. The ministry can grind you down. I was in a mountain area during the Christmas holidays after a season of draining work. I decided to go up in the mountains for one night to pray. No food, just water. I had a tent and warm clothes. Where I live in New York City, sirens wail day and night. Horns honk, brakes squeal. I thought I would love the silence of the woods in winter.

Finally, I was alone in the woods. But as often happens, instead of finding inner peace, all my personal demons started rising up within me—grudges from the past, failures, things I should have said, things I should have done. It felt like torture.

I tried to distract myself by building a fire in the cold, which made me feel a little better. As the darkness and the cold deepened, I realized I was probably the only human for miles around. I was shocked at the silence. It felt as though the whole planet was cold and dead. I don't get to camp very much. I'd never heard a hoot owl before. Its spooky call in a tree, breaking the total winter silence, started freaking me out. I didn't really know what it was. I started missing the horns of the taxis.

So inner tranquility eluded me. I finally went to bed in the tent, eyes wide open, fighting off feelings of inferiority, fear, and disquiet. After midnight, I heard rustling in the leaves. A large animal loped up to my tent and began to sniff around. It sure sounded larger than a raccoon. Was it just a dog, a coyote, a wolf, a bear? I made the decision not to stick my head out to find out. It walked around my tent sniffing. In my toughest voice, I shouted, "Get out of here!" The creature sauntered off—it didn't seem particularly scared. As it rustled the leaves in the woods, it sounded huge—more like an elephant than a squirrel.

The night dragged on. All the normal to-do lists were gone. But instead of peace, I felt anger and fear. The cold hours stretched on unbearably. Finally, I decided I would get up in the middle of the night, break camp, and climb a mountain trail toward the east so I could see the sunrise. If the sunrise would ever come.

I hiked along in the dark, hoping I wouldn't meet my nocturnal visitor again. It's funny what loneliness, cold, and a little stillness can do to you. Every sound—a broken stick, a movement in the bushes—made me jump like a scared puppy. There was enough moonlight that I didn't need a flashlight.

Why wasn't this prayer time what I thought it would be? As I walked, I began to hear footsteps behind me, clear footsteps, and close by. I stopped. The steps continued for a moment, and then they stopped too. I started again. Close by I heard the steps again. My body was a racetrack for adrenaline. I stopped again. The footsteps continued for a moment and then also stopped. I started running along the trail, in the dark. The footsteps behind me picked up their pace too. I ran faster. It's funny where your bravery goes when you are all alone on a cold mountain at 4:00 in the morning.

I turned around. I heard movement behind me again. I turned around again. It wasn't there. Finally it dawned on me. In my backpack, the water in my water bottle had partially frozen. The chunks had started sloshing around every time I took a step. It took the ice a moment to stop sloshing when I stopped moving. I felt ridiculous. I laughed a snorty laugh, the kind of laugh you make when you are all alone.

Somehow my time changed after that. I began to see a tiny bit of light on the farthest rim of the horizon. I didn't mind anymore the slosh of ice behind me. With lists of things to do stripped away, I began to remember the reason I was in the city, the reason I was doing what I was doing. God can be subtle, but God can also be a heavy-handed symbolizer—and certainly through nature. As the sun came up over the mountains, slowly my reason for working in New York dawned on me again. But I wouldn't have known it if I had just kept working harder in the city. I wouldn't have known it if I hadn't sought out a time to strip away the normal.

A Full Garden or a Single Flower

Sometimes stripping away cargo can just mean being alone. The enclosing room that seems so limiting is not. The four walls turn out to only be three walls. We find the enclosure opens up into a realm we had not expected. We have in the New Testament the letters we call the prison epistles—Ephesians, Colossians, Philippians, and Philemon. These are the ones we know Paul wrote in prison. However, the limits that were placed on Paul didn't seem to limit him. These letters have some of Paul's deepest insights and most expansive views.

John of Patmos was supposedly stuck in a cave on a prisoner's island. Yet he saw the unseen open up to him in a profound way and wrote about the end of space and time as we know it and about a new heaven and a new earth where God will wipe every tear from our eyes. The Book of Revelation is his record of what he saw. The cave could not enclose him.

Insights come from limitations. After writing his famous "Letter from Birmingham Jail," Martin Luther King Jr. described how he wrote the letter: "Begun on the margins of the newspaper in which the statement appeared while I was in jail, the letter was continued on scraps of writing paper supplied by a friendly black trusty, and concluded on a pad my attorneys were eventually permitted to leave me." Written in the margins of a newspaper, scraps, and a notepad, the letter gave a reason for the way the movement moved forward. Students read the letter in anthologies in nearly every public school now.

Limitations from our normal life, lack of the resources we are accustomed to, lack of the basic amenities—some people realize such limitations give a certain kind of freedom. Henry David Thoreau was an American poet who saw this simplicity in his own way. As he lived alone at Walden Pond he wrote, "I had three pieces of limestone on my desk, but I was terrified to find that they required to be dusted daily, when the furniture of my mind was all undusted still, and I threw them out the window in disgust." Keep things simple.

Perhaps one of the main purposes of art is to help us limit our focus in order to expand our lives. A simple vase of sunflowers in the hand of an artist like Vincent van Gogh becomes a window into an entire way of seeing the world.

As a missionary in Hong Kong many years ago, I heard a lot of stories from the East. One of the most well-known Japanese stories involves Rikyu, a famous tea master from the sixteenth century. Rikyu planted morning glories in his Kyoto garden, and the tyrannical shogun in the area heard of the extreme beauty of the blooms. The military dictator announced he would bring his retinue from his castle to Rikyu's simple tea hut in order to view the flowers.

When the shogun arrived, he found that all the morning glories in the garden had been removed, roots and all. Furious at this insult, he entered Rikyu's small teahouse. There the shogun found one perfect morning glory, shining with dew, set in a simple bamboo container in a small alcove. Slowly, the shogun began to grasp the meaning of Rikyu's generous gesture, and Rikyu entered the room.

It's an eastern story, and so it has a lot of meanings. But part of the meaning must involve Rikyu's conscious limitation so that the shogun could really appreciate a morning glory and not just see a garden full of flowers. In the context, the story is also about risk, because Rikyu risks his life to share something with someone who might misunderstand and had the power to kill him at once with a simple command.

Focus on one thing, not a hundred things. This sentiment may be a part of the reason why Jesus said, "Any of you who does not renounce all that he has cannot be my disciple" (Luke 14:33). Saying no to many things helps us to say yes to the most important thing. Some Christians talk about the interior stripping that goes on as we follow Christ, a process that matches the exterior limitation—the inner and the outer wilderness.

A CRACK IN THE WALL

So a desert experience can strip you. Even a time in the wilderness—the modern equivalent might be camping in the wild—deprives you of many of the things you value. No cell phone service, no restrooms, no refrigerator, no microwave, no remote control. It helps us see what we could not see before.

Richard Byrd, the admiral who helped explore the Antarctic, had to leave many normal comforts behind in order to explore new territories. He made this comment once in his diary: "I am learning . . . that a man can live profoundly without masses of things."

Masses of things. Paul is in prison, but he prays for the people in the churches, and in a way, he prays for us. He himself is in prison, but in his prayer he uses a distinctive phrase. He prays that the "eyes of your hearts" might be "enlightened" (Ephesians 1:18). In the end, it isn't an exterior thing. It is an interior thing, seen from the heart. In some ways, it is the way we approach it.

TAKEAWAY:

1. Sometimes you can look for the grand and miss the wonderful.

2. Paradoxically, increasing limitation can bring an expansion of vision.

3. By deliberately unplugging, we find ourselves plugged into what is more important.

10

EMPTYING IN
ORDER TO BE FULL

He thought, or said, or sang, I did not know
that I was so empty, to be so full.

—Peter S. Beagle, *The Last Unicorn*

*This is a strange place to be, isn't it, John?
You've lost everything; you live in a cave on
a prison island. You cannot leave or do what
you want. You are separated from your family,
your church, your friends. You're old. You can't
do what you used to do. Isn't it odd? It is here,
in captivity, that you have seen the grandness
of the vision of the new heaven and the new
earth, of abundance, of Jesus telling all to come
who are thirsty. Who would have guessed it?
Certainly not your captors.*

BEING HOLLOW IN ORDER TO RING

Expansion beyond the limitation. Fullness beyond the emptiness. Panoramas through the cracks of a jail cell wall. This is the oddness of life, the life of Hagar, Joseph, Jeremiah, Paul, of John. John is trapped on an island off the coast of Turkey. He didn't plan to be there. Tradition has it he was enclosed in a cave on the side of a mountain. From an outside view, he seems to have lost everything—the power to go where he wants, the ability to be with his church community, his family, and his friends. So much to do as the last surviving apostle and so little he could do, at least externally. I wonder what it felt like as he woke up every day, looking out of the sea that separated him from all those who were dear to him. Perhaps he felt separated from his purpose too—to help the believers in his church.

Yet it is here in the place of deprivation that John has his vision, his revelation, as the Bible calls it. Revelation seems to be a book that tries to utter the unutterable, to run against the walls of language with images beyond our comprehension—angels and choruses and those who have died and rainbow colors and thrones and severe judgment on the bullies in this world, all with code words used when one is in prison and oppressed.

Finally in this revelation, there is a vision of a city, inexpressively tall, inexplicably wonderful, where all the physical separations and worldly trappings of religious activity are gone, where there is no temple or even need of sun or moon, where "the glory of God gives it light" (Revelation 21:23). In the end, Jesus, the one who is both lion and lamb, calls out to all who have been empty or thirsty. "Come," he says, so that anyone that is thirsty can drink of the water of life. These are Jesus' final words in the Bible (Revelation 22:6–21).

This understanding is that same great paradox of life we have been discussing—fullness that comes out of emptiness. Of course, in a way, we all know about emptiness and fullness deep inside. We don't really want to be a solid cube if we want to receive. We are more of a bowl, which must be empty in order to receive. We're made to be a bowl, not a closed box. A bell must be hollow in order to sound the peel that is needed to be heard. Oddly enough, sometimes we need to be aware of our emptiness before we can be full.

In the Bible God teaches us of our own need. At one point, He reminds us of our own bondage and then instructs us in the way to something different: "I am the LORD your God, who brought you up out of the land of Egypt. Open your mouth wide, and I will fill it" (Psalm 81:10).

One man in our mission understood the journey of stripping away and then the coming of the new. When we were going through a difficult time, he was not discouraged. He simply said, "We are cleaning the plate in order for the steak to come."

Why is there such richness in emptiness? I remember one of the first Christmases we had at our mission. We were in a storefront, and many of the buildings on our street were still abandoned, yet filled with the homeless, the mentally ill, and the addicted. We were having hot chocolate and playing old Christmas hymns in a room smaller than a garage. The place smelled like a thrift shop. A ragtag group drifted in and out. Where else could they go? They had layers of coats on and smelled of old clothing and smoke, since they were warming themselves by illegal fires on the street, often built in old trash cans.

Yet there was no self-pity, no whimpering. There was an odd joy—even though no one had gifts to exchange. There was also that quality of humor, which I often saw in those who had the least. One particularly angry man, who ranted about the horrors of the American system and had alienated just about everyone on the street, came in with a scowl.

As we sat and drank hot chocolate, we could still see our breath, though we were inside the storefront. The heater wasn't working so well and smelled a bit of gasoline. The man took a sip from the hot cup and told the group why he came here instead of going to a large place downtown that dealt with thousands of needy people. "Well, I finally decided I would rather be with people I know and don't like, than be with people I don't know and don't like." For some reason, we all found this quite funny, and we all cackled in a grizzly way, keeping out coats wrapped tightly around our necks.

Why do I treasure that Christmas morning more than many others where we had so much more abundance? For that matter, why do older married couples talk with such joy about their early days when they didn't have any money and had to scrounge even to survive? What is this bare irregularity that makes emptiness feel like fullness?

THE MAN WHO HATED THE PEG AND THE MAN WHO LOVED IT

In a deeper way, this fullness even reaches through that final limitation—death. For much of my adult life, I lived thousands of miles away from my mother. I was in large urban areas, and she lived in a small town. She poured her life into her five children, but she was also a painter. So much of who I am is because of her. When she died, strangely enough, I felt her presence even more clearly. Her love of life and beauty seemed to pervade my thinking in a new way as I savored the trees, the wind, the skies— things so dear to her that she painted so often. In that way, her death became an expansion, as those who loved her sensed life in an even larger way.

Sometimes we are given a choice. We are given a chance to choose the desert, the stripping away. As mentioned before, this is even called the "emptying" approach to life. The word for *empty* in Greek is *kenoó*, so the fancy way to talk about this approach is "kenotic theology." The approach comes from a time in Paul's life when he was in jail. Some of the people he was writing to were apparently experiencing envy and rivalry. He tells them to choose another attitude, the attitude of Christ, who emptied Himself, or "made himself nothing" (Philippians 2:7 NIV). It is important to mention, however, that in the end of the passage, things are once again turned upside down. Christ, who empties Himself, becomes highly exalted.

Many people from many cultures talk about being empty, and it can mean many things. But this emptying of Christ never seems to be simply having some experience of greater vision of self-realization. It always seems to emphasize a pouring out, an emptying for the sake of others. This theme runs through the whole Bible, not just through the life of Christ. In Isaiah 58:10, the prophet said to "pour yourself out for the hungry and satisfy the desire of the afflicted." Ironically, then your light will "rise in the darkness, and your gloom be as the noonday." So this process of emptying can never be only a journey for self-realization. Without the goal of helping others, it becomes self-centered and can only take the person deeper into a vacant well of mirrors.

This inversion of values—emptying in order to be full, is hard to describe in a linear way. Artists try to do so sometimes. The Christian apologist G. K. Chesterton wrote much about Christ and the Christian approach to life. Sometimes he wrote novels. In *The Ball and the Cross*, a self-proclaimed atheist finds himself imprisoned in a cell in an asylum. On one wall, there is an iron peg that seems to have no reason or object. The man is trapped with nothing else in the cell. He comes to hate that peg with a deep hatred.

Eventually the atheist is able to encounter a man who is in a different cell. That other cell is similar, but the prisoner seems content and joyful. He points to the same projection from his own cell, the iron peg, and proclaims that the spike is the best thing about his cell. The atheist concludes that the other prisoner is either an idiot or a madman. The reader is left to make his or her own conclusions. For one man, the empty cell with its peg was a hell. For the other, the cell with that peg was a heaven. Incidentally, the other prisoner offers to help, and the iron doors are then found unlocked.

In Philippians 3:17–18, Paul tries to describe this joy when he is confined to a cell. He says when we are grounded in love, we may be able to comprehend far beyond our normal perceptions "with all the saints what is the breadth and length and height and depth." We will "know the love of Christ that surpasses knowledge." Strange things to say in jail when you are facing execution. All of this will happen, he says, "that you may be filled with all the fullness of God." The fullness of God. One could hardly think larger than this.

WHAT DO WE REALLY VALUE?

Whether in a place of confinement or destitution, in a desert or a wilderness, we sometimes must move to a choice. In the end, these choices probably won't be made unless we have a habit of making them. How could David possibly make the choices he made as he was a middle-aged man in a desert running for his life, betrayed by his son, and facing total humiliation, not to mention death? What kept him from despair when he was forced to leave the comforts of the palace and live in the wastelands again?

David uses the very dryness of the waterless place as a springboard for song to God. As we read the lyrics of the songs in Psalms, we see he made this a habit. He made these physical deprivations a way to praise God. While in the wilderness, David expressed, "My soul thirsts for you; my flesh faints for you, as in a dry and weary land where there is no water" (Psalm 63:1). What is this puzzling fullness in the darker moments of life?

Choosing to rejoice in the midst of emptiness was probably a habit for both David in the Old Testament and for Paul in the New Testament. While in jail, Paul instructed the brothers and sisters in Christ to "rejoice in the Lord always" (Philippians 4:4). He gave them instructions and assumed they could choose to do so, and to do it always. He was in jail, and he was rejoicing. He said he had learned to be content, to face "abundance and need" (v. 12). It doesn't always happen, but there is a strange fullness in the midst of unspeakable hardship.

In the seventeenth century, Brother Lawrence lived a life of limitation and emptying. He worked in a kitchen in a religious community. He had a lowly job, washing pots and pans. Yet he had such peace that people sought him out. We have the record of some of his conversations. How could he have such richness and fullness?

Brother Lawrence wrote of the flow of God's graces, which is like a torrent. However, he points out something that is a great insight. He says we often stop this flow of abundance. The way we stop it is by not valuing it.

Of course, our own generation is barraged by information and entertainment and preoccupations. Technology hasn't really given us more time for leisure and wonder, but it has often increased our tension. Brother Lawrence, who lived so long ago, may in actuality have simple instructions that are crucial for us to know—instructions to intentionally value that flow of God's presence. It is a good challenge—does the constant flow of trivial communication keep us from choosing to value that far more important flow of God's presence? Perhaps we are sometimes only able to choose such real valuing when the things in our life, the unending torrent of stuff, are limited by circumstances beyond our control.

TO BE SO EMPTY TO BE SO FULL

In the end, the desert, the wilderness, the wasteland, or any place of deprivation, brings us again to this intuitive, nonverbal, nonlinear paradox. Our deepest pleasures and fullness sometimes become most distinct in the midst of want and hardship. No one seeks it out, but then again, there it is. Somehow, love mingled with hardship grows even greater.

At the beginning of the chapter, I quoted from a fairy story written decades ago that is addressing a time of cynicism and disbelief. One of the characters says, "I did not know that I was so empty, to be so full." Again and again, we find this experience in the biblical story. So empty to be so full. Fullness is not earned. We can't really schedule it or plan its timing. It's not that kind of thing. Stories in life don't necessarily go the way we want to shape them, do they? Perhaps this is part of the wisdom of the desert too.

After working for more than forty years with people in deep need in urban areas, I still can't explain why so many people I worked with had such deep hardship, yet lived such full and rich lives. Their sense of humor, grittiness, and unselfishness only humbles me. As I look at them, I find I have nothing to brag about in my own life. Yet there is no guarantee such a turn of events will happen. Many other people I worked with ended in despair, bitterness, rage, and inner defeat. I don't think I can ever really explain it, but to me, this is the way of the world.

I am thinking right now of one of the men I work with. I have known him for a long, long time. I watched phases in his life when he stole, alienated his family, descended into betrayal and crack addiction, was forced into rehab, betrayed people again, and made promises to Christians and failed to follow through. Yet somehow, through that wilderness of his life, he became strong in those broken places.

I see him now, helping so many people, being a leader, always fulfilling his promises, and being someone I deeply admire. Sometimes in the middle of a tough day—maybe someone with mental illness has cursed us out, maybe stole something from us at the mission, something more than we offered—his calmness, his assurance, and his understanding makes me realize how much further I have to go. In those times, I remind him of a verse I claim for him, one from the prophet Joel: "I will restore to you the years that the swarming locust have eaten" (2:25). I saw it happen. You can't make something like this up. Those years, eaten away by loss, have been restored even more fully.

People who choose limitation for the sake of others somehow make us stop and think deeply about why we are here. Jesus did it. Paul says, "though he was rich, yet for your sake he became poor, so that you by his poverty might become rich" (2 Corinthians 8:9). Why did He do so? What does that mean as I live my life?

PEACE BY CLEANING TOILETS

One of the people who taught me first about expansion I met as a teenager. From the beginning, he wanted to be a writer. He wrote stories all the time. His family was far different from mine. Mine was strict in many ways with clear boundaries. There was no alcohol in our house. I was surprised when I went to his house that he could pull a beer out of the refrigerator, even as a young teenager, and drink as he wrote. His mom didn't mind.

He wanted to write more than anything. When I visited him, he'd recommend titles for me to read. He found himself rather out of touch with the majority culture in an Oklahoman high school at the time. He approached those differences, and his exclusion from the cool groups, with self-deprecating humor.

As we left high school, our paths diverged. He became a Jesus freak at one point, while I decided I didn't believe in God. Later he examined his own sexual orientation and explored a lot of different lifestyles in San Francisco. He was often unhappy.

But when I last saw him, I noticed a strange peace about him. With all his intelligence and writing ability, he had chosen to work in the lowest paying job, in a large dismal state institute for the developmentally challenged. I think he cleaned the toilets. The nine-to-five job gave him time to write, and the limited income gave him an opportunity to simplify. He was writing a lot, and his writing was getting better and better. His journey with God was deeper, more thoughtful. That was the last time I saw him.

Later I heard the news that one Sunday morning, he was driving back from a friend's house on a lonely stretch of road, and he fell asleep. His car hit a concrete abutment. He died instantly. He was thirty years old.

My friend never became the great writer he longed to be. He never got famous with published books. It has now been more than thirty years since he died. Yet his inverted values live on in others. I find myself thinking about him, his gentle generosity, his sense of humor, his imagination, and his final choice, against all perceptions, to simply serve others. I think about things he said, his thoughts, and his writings. In a sense, his ending was one of sad limitation.

Yet through it, a strange fullness emerged and has kept growing in me and in others.

Perhaps Paul understood this. In 2 Corinthians, he began to brag about his weakness. He began to brag about a prayer request he continued to make, one that seemed unanswered. Yet this strange, seemingly unanswered prayer, this request from an apostle that comes back empty, doesn't really come back empty. God answers him after he prays three times for an answer. God does not remove the thing that has been plaguing Paul, as Paul requested. Instead, God says, "my power is made perfect in weakness" (2 Corinthians 12:9).

Paul got it and tried the best he could to impart this insight to the people in his local church and ultimately to us. Paul said, "When I am weak, then I am strong" (v. 10). He found strength in the odd story of Christ. Christ "was crucified in weakness, but lives by the power of God" (13:4). In one sense, the inversion of values—weakness and power, emptiness and fullness—seems illogical. But in another sense, in life, it seems so real.

How, we ask, could emptiness ever bring hope? It has happened before. We read the stories of Jesus, the stories after He was brutally executed. As His friends sought to tie loose ends up, as they grieved, they found emptiness. It is personified in the discovery of the empty tomb. Is this not one more grief added to unspeakable grief? Is this final story of deserted emptiness not a mockery of all He stood for? Did someone move the body without permission, or did the authorities relocate it, or did some cynical thieves steal it? This is the paradox of the Christian story. For from this great emptiness comes that greatest hope.

TAKEAWAY:

1. Oddly enough, emptiness often creates the space for fullness in life.

2. Choosing to empty yourself for others can become the walk of life.

3. For David, the dryness of the desert becomes a springboard for praise.

4. Paul became strong by becoming weak.

CONCLUSION

A PROCESS, NOT AN ADDRESS

If you're going through hell . . . don't slow down.

—Rodney Atkins

So it has come to this, has it? You've gone through Your whole life helping others, but where are they now? Now You're all alone, aren't You? Let's face it—people don't care that much, not even Your friends. All Your work, even Your whole life, seems kind of wasted tonight, when You really think about it. You're going to die soon. They will put their hands upon You. It will be painful, and then You will be dead. You always knew this would happen. Your time here didn't end up in fulfillment. It ended up in this. This is a garden, but tonight, when You are all alone, it feels like a desert, doesn't it? Calm down. Why are You sweating so much, Jesus?

I'M IN A WASTELAND

When we are feeling lost in life, I suppose that the Bible can give us an accurate diagnosis of things—sometimes we need that. But for me, it gives something more important. The Bible also gives us stories. We read about people who were lost and confused and didn't know which way to go. Sometimes we are allowed to hear the peoples' prayers in their most difficult times, filled with desperation or joy or both. Sometimes we get to read the lyrics of the songs they wrote. These stories aren't formulaic. They don't always have happy endings. They don't feel like instruction manuals. Perhaps most importantly, we walk away from the stories with metaphors for our own lives. "I'm in a desert," or "I'm in a wasteland." "Man, this is like a wilderness."

As we have often noted, in the first stories in the Bible, people were sometimes literally in a desert, a barren uncharted area. But in the end, the people of God were able to take that metaphor to many places. At the end of Jesus' life, He was in a garden—the garden of Gethsemane. We know it was tough. He asked His closest friends to stay up with Him, but they didn't. The Bible says His perspiration was like drops of blood. It was the end of His earthly life, but it certainly didn't feel like the Promised Land.

We have looked at the paradox of the wilderness—its bleakness and its richness. It is a place of seeming purposelessness, sometimes dishonor, invisibility, stripping away, and uncertain waiting. It is also a place of deep insight, learned humility, and fuller vision. But we have also seen that in the Bible, the wilderness is never a destination. It is something we must go through.

We start in a garden in Genesis. We end in a wondrous, healing city in the Book of Revelation. The wilderness is simply one of the in-between times. We watch this movement from the desert to the Promised Land. Eventually, we can understand many experiences, internal or external, as desert experiences. We often see that basic movement from wilderness to new land in our own lives—the continuing movement from suffering to insight.

From the early books in the Bible, the desert or wilderness becomes a sign for us—it is something we go through. Still, whether the time is long or short, the Promised Land is on the other side.

Such an insight has a practical application in our work here now. Grief and that sense of purposelessness are a process. They are not an address. We want to go through "the valley of the shadow of death" (Psalm 23:4). We don't want to build our permanent residence there. Some people try. They formalize their grief or their confusion or their heartache—they make that experience the definition of who they are—forever. One can get stuck in a phase—fixed in one experience, unable to move forward. Perhaps that is what hell is like.

I have worked in urban areas for more than forty years and with people in New York City who are homeless and often alcoholics for more than thirty of those. I have heard many, many stories. I am amazed at how often people who are currently drinking disastrously will claim the reason they are doing so is something that happened many years before. They lost a loved one. They had a horrible heart condition as a child. Their spouse left. It doesn't occur to them that their drinking has become their address. Grieving is important, yet some have framed their hardship on their most prominent wall, and they simply cannot look away from it.

Even when the people of God build a temple in their wilderness experience in Exodus, it is not something that is permanent or fixed. It is in reality a sort of moveable tent—its structure makes the physical statement that they are going somewhere. In Exodus, even the manna the people ate in the desert, the flakes that appeared each morning, was there to get them through the desert. The people were in survival mode. This manna stopped coming once they had the abundant food they found in their next phase of life.

When you are going through a difficult situation, keep moving. Don't fixate on that one phase. Don't lay your permanent foundation there, with a sewage system and a street number. Don't make it your address.

ARE WE GREATER THAN WE KNOW?

Here's the challenge. From this perspective, one might think we would find an amazing abundance for people in the Bible at the end of their lives. Sometimes this is the result, but it's not always necessarily so. Moses, the master of the wilderness, did not even make it to the Promised Land. He died alone with God on a mountain (Deuteronomy 34). Jeremiah was taken forcibly to Egypt at the end of his life by leaders who continued to refuse to listen to his counsel (Jeremiah 43). Jesus was betrayed by His own followers and asked God that He not have to go through the kind of death He had to face (Luke 22). Paul, at the end of his life, was deserted by those he thought would defend him (2 Timothy 4). John was forcibly held on an island and cut off from his community (Revelation 1).

Still, being in that kind of wilderness makes us ask the deeper questions too. What if things don't work out in this life? Things so often don't. As a pastor in New York City, I have performed funerals for many different kinds of people. I recently participated in a funeral for a young man who was shot on the street as part of a gang. His gang was there in force at the funeral home. They seemed to be angry at everyone. Of course, anger often masks fear. They were angry at the family, angry at the funeral director, angry at life, angry at me for what I might represent. Everything provoked a silent anger—the open casket, the young man's good-looking face, the heavy silence, the sickly smell of funeral flowers in a crowded room, the open book for people to sign, the feeling of helplessness, the semidarkness except for where the casket was, the soft moaning in the corners.

Yet strangely enough, at a funeral home, we all are together in a unique way too. In a sense, no matter who we are, we are all in the same boat. Regardless of our background, we all have to ask some of the most basic questions. An unusual bond occurs there.

What happens when we die? What is the reason for this strange handful of decades we have of consciousness in this life? Is this all there is? Is there some kind of bigger purpose, or is this all just material happenstance?

Then who are we? The quiet in a funeral home forces the questions in some form, no matter who we are, even if only for a few minutes. Every pastor knows that.

Or is there something more? Are we more than just chemical scum? Each person has to answer that question for him or herself. Regardless of our foundational views, we somehow feel as though there is something more, but we don't know how to say it. Is another poet, William Wordsworth, right when he said, "We feel that we are greater than we know"?

Greater than we know. Perhaps. The wilderness tends to strip away the clutter of our normal lives. The illusion of temporary goals and routines seem far more important at the time than they really are. The wilderness helps us ask—are we related in life to something infinite, or is all our experience finite and limited? For me, without the context of eternity, much of what is in the Bible, and really, much of what is in our life, remains a riddle. Moses died unfulfilled. Jeremiah was unsuccessful. Paul was abandoned in jail.

But many issues and questions change if we put our little lives in the context of something beyond ourselves.

EXILES HEADING SOMEWHERE

If we are just little ants on a huge basketball, circling the sun for a pocketful of years, then much of our deepest yearnings seem rather inconsequential. Times of wilderness, times of purposelessness—well, they come and go. It doesn't really matter.

Even if we live to old age, we face our own special kind of desert—an increasing stripping of who we are. Our friends, our health, and our minds all can go. We can find ourselves, as Shakespeare says, in the final stage of life, without teeth, without eyes, without taste, without everything.

Is this experience of life in some ways simply an experience of random purposelessness, or is there really a destination? The Bible says there is a reason for the traveling. Hebrews describes the people of faith, people who walk with a conviction of things not seen. They don't have everything all figured out. Still, these are the people who have acknowledged that we are "strangers and exiles on this earth" (Hebrews 11:13). They are headed for a destination—"seeking a homeland" (v. 14). In the end, with all the grief and challenges of this world, and even meaningless death, they "desire a better country, that is, a heavenly one" (v. 16). In the context of eternity, God can "wipe away every tear from their eyes" (Revelation 21:4).

This is part of the paradox of the wandering in the wilderness. Once we look at so much in this life—the seeming randomness of much of the suffering, the meaninglessness of much of our preoccupations, the inexplicable heartache of the death of a child, the unfairness of many careers or even the lack of a career—we are confronted in all of its purposelessness. Yet in the wasteland, when things are taken away from us, we sometimes see beyond our little lives, our petty pawing for attention and comfort, even beyond death. Then sometimes we do sense we are greater than we know. This special sense may be the greatest gift of the desert.

We started the chapter with Jesus in a time of heartache and a time of prayerful searching. To be honest, as we look at the story itself in earthly terms, Jesus didn't really do anything practical to help anyone when He died. He didn't jump in front a rushing chariot to save a child; He didn't step in front of a man being beaten to death and take the blows for Him. He was simply abandoned by His friends and betrayed. He was horribly humiliated. In one sense, He died an unfair, meaningless, pathetic, senseless death. The end of His life looked like just another wilderness.

Once again, those who had the gold made the rules. In the end, the halls of political power and the circles of petty religious influence won, as they always do, crushing an innocent man who came to help others. Yes, those visible material powers triumphed once more.

Yet, strangely enough, they didn't.

TAKEAWAY:

1. The wilderness experience is a process, not an address.

2. The end of our life could be another wilderness experience, instead of the expected time of fulfillment.

3. Our view changes when we see our lives from the context of eternity.

Discussion Questions ⎯⎯⎯⎯

Introduction—The Wilderness as Paradox

Sometimes we enter a wilderness time when we are hit by more than one hardship at once. Can you describe a time in your life when you found difficulty on several fronts at one time? What helped you get through it?

Have you ever been in a time of struggle and someone said the wrong thing to you when they tried to help? How did that make you feel? Do you think you have ever given a "formula answer" to someone else inappropriately? Why do you think you did it?

Read Psalm 107:4–5. Have you ever felt really lost, literally or figuratively? Did you learn anything from the experience?

Read Matthew 10:39. Why do you think Jesus makes statements that sound contradictory? Do these statements point to some quality in our lives?

PRINCIPLE #1: HONORING DISHONOR

Can you think of a time when you felt embarrassed or humiliated? Why do you think those experiences are so hard for us?

Do you think it is true we sometimes learn humility through humiliation? Why or why not?

Read Genesis 21:1–6. Why do you think Sarah would name her child a name that sounded like "laugh"? What kind of statement do you think she was trying to make?

Humiliation can kill a person or lead them to a deeper relationship with God. What makes the difference?

PRINCIPLE #2: BECOMING A NOBODY

Have you ever felt invisible? Can you describe how you felt? Can we learn anything from the experience?

Read Genesis 40:20–23. The chief cupbearer didn't hate Joseph; he just forgot him. What's the difference? Which experience is worse—being hated or being forgotten?

In certain contexts, people can feel ignored because they are too young and inexperienced or ignored because they are too old and out-of-date. Is there anyone in your sphere of influence who might feel that way? What can you learn from them?

In Philippians 2:5–8 (NIV), Paul says that Jesus "made himself nothing." Why do you think Jesus needed to make Himself nothing?

PRINCIPLE #3: FINDING YOUR UNCERTAINTY

Have you ever had an experience when you just didn't know what to do? If so, what was the worst part of the experience?

How do you personally handle times when you don't know what to do? What helps you get through those times?

Read Genesis 21:8–21. Hagar did not know what to do and had quit in despair. What did God do to assist her? Did

He remove her from the desert? How has God assisted you when you didn't know what to do?

Have your times of uncertainty ever helped you understand and know God better? If so, how?

PRINCIPLE #4: SUBTRACTING RATHER THAN ADDING

Recall one time when you experienced subtraction in your life. Were there any pluses that came out of it?

Did losing something in your life ever feel eventually like a liberation? Why or why not?

Read Philippians 3:4–11. What does Paul lose, and what does he gain?

Have you ever had the experience of losing something in life and as a consequence become more appreciative of what you do have? Why and how do you think that happens?

PRINCIPLE #5: GIVING UP INSTEAD OF GIVING IN

Have you had a time in your life when you prayed for something and you didn't get it? How did you handle that time?

Are you the type of person who has a lot of persistence, or grit? How did you develop it, or what kept you from developing it?

Read a bit of the story of Caleb as an old man in Joshua 14:6–15 (if you want, you can read a bit of his story as a younger man in Numbers 13:25—14:10). What qualities does he have that could help the younger generation survive?

Right now, do you see yourself more as a hero in the middle of your own adventure or as a *senex* helping someone else through their adventure? Explain why.

PRINCIPLE #6: FAILING OVER SUCCEEDING

What is one area of your life where you feel you have failed? What other emotions for you accompanied that failure?

Talk about David Brooks's comment, that success leads to the greatest failure—pride, and failure leads to the greatest success—humility. How is that true or not true in your life?

Read Jeremiah 20:14–18. Did Jeremiah feel like a failure? Was Jeremiah a failure?

Catherine Doherty likens an empty room with nothing but a bed and a Bible to a desert. Do you feel you ever need a desert time to simply sort your life out with God? Why or why not?

PRINCIPLE #7: DEVELOPING WAIT TRAINING

What would you say if God were to ask you, "What are you waiting for?" Does your waiting have a known deadline or is it open-ended? What is the hardest part about waiting for you?

In the end, do you think your spiritual life was weakened or strengthened by a time of waiting? Why?

Look at a part of Abraham and Sarah's story in Genesis 15:1–3. Do you sense a note of frustration in Abraham's prayer? How do you think this delay in the promise changed Abraham?

Can you remember a time in your life when a prayer seemed unanswered but was later answered richly in a way you did not expect?

PRINCIPLE #8: REFUSING TO MAKE THINGS HAPPEN

What type of person are you? Are you the type that likes to make things happen, or are you the type that likes to allow things to happen? Explain your answer.

Have you ever had to pray a prayer of relinquishment? What was the result? If you haven't prayed this kind of prayer before, share a bit about what your prayers are like.

Read John 21:18–19. Why do you think Jesus said these words to Peter? Can you think of a time in your journey when life itself helped you to allow things to happen rather than to make things happen? Do you see experiences ahead of you that might help you learn to do so?

When you encounter a frustrating or difficult experience, do you tend to move faster and faster or go slower and slower? Why?

PRINCIPLE #9: FINDING THE LITTLE VISION OVER THE BIG VISION

Can you describe a time when hardship helped you see beyond yourself to understand others better?

Do you see a connection between the number of material goods a person has and their sense of well-being? Why or why not?

Zechariah 4:6–10 is a passage that can be difficult to understand. Read it in several translations. The people are discouraged because the work isn't going faster and the Temple isn't grander. It seemed like a day of small things. Can you describe a time when you expected things to move faster and be bigger and in the process you missed what God was doing?

Jesus says that to be His disciple we must renounce all we have (Luke 14:33). What might that mean for you in your context? What might that kind of focus help you see?

PRINCIPLE #10: EMPTYING IN ORDER TO BE FULL

What treasured memories occurred in the midst of hardship or want?

Why do you think some people are content and some people are not? Do you think you have to learn contentment, or does it just happen with some personalities?

Read Revelation 22:1–5. Do you think John's vision would have been so clear if he had not been in a situation of deprivation? Why or why not?

Some people take their intense hardship and turn it into something that can help others. Others rage against God and their situation and die in resentment. What do you think makes the difference?

CONCLUSION: A PROCESS, NOT AN ADDRESS

Some of the places in the Bible become used as metaphors, such as the Garden of Eden, the wilderness, or the Promised Land. What metaphor or comparison would you use to describe the phase you are in now? Could you use one of the three we mentioned, or would you use another comparison?

We stated that grieving can be a process and not necessarily an address. Do you think that statement is true? Why or why not? Are you in a process of grieving now? What is helping you get through? If you are not grieving, are you noticing anything that has helped your friends get through that tough process?

Read Hebrews 11:13–16. This passage describes some of the heroes of faith in the Bible, and they are described as exiles here on earth. Where are they heading? How does the Bible describe their destination? How would you describe your destination?

The Bible states that Jesus' life didn't stop on the day of His Crucifixion. What difference does that make for you?

ABOUT GRAFFITI

Graffiti Community Ministry started in a storefront forty years ago. Now it works to express God's love in tangible ways for thousands each year. Since that time, it has expanded to include Graffiti 2 in the South Bronx, Graffiti 3 in Brooklyn, Gotta Serve in Long Island, and Graffiti Coney Island. Graffiti has affiliates in Baltimore, Philadelphia, and Chicago. It has fostered and supported more than sixty new churches while acting as mother church, aunt church, or grandmother church. It also partners with a number of ministries in New York City in a commitment to do the small things to serve the unserved. For more information, contact Graffiti Community Ministry by mail at 205 E. 7th Street, New York, NY 10009, by phone at 212-473-0044, or online at graffitichurch.org. To learn more about Graffiti's Upside-Down training, visit upsidedownlife.org.

If you enjoyed this book, will you consider sharing the message with others?

Let us know your thoughts at info@newhopepublishers.com. You can also let the author know by visiting or sharing a photo of the cover on our social media pages or leaving a review at a retailer's site. All of it helps us get the message out!

Twitter.com/NewHopeBooks

Facebook.com/NewHopePublishers

Instagram.com/NewHopePublishers

———————

New Hope® Publishers is a division of Iron Stream Media, which derives its name from Proverbs 27:17, "As iron sharpens iron, so one person sharpens another."

This sharpening describes the process of discipleship, one to another. With this in mind, Iron Stream Media provides a variety of solutions for churches, missionaries, and nonprofits ranging from in-depth Bible study curriculum and Christian book publishing to custom publishing and consultative services. Through the popular Life Bible Study and Student Life Bible Study brands, ISM provides web-based full-year and short-term Bible study teaching plans as well as printed devotionals, Bibles, and discipleship curriculum.

For more information on ISM and New Hope Publishers, please visit

IronStreamMedia.com

NewHopePublishers.com